Rick: My Dad hasn't slept for *twelve* days, but he isn't a bit tired.
Dick: Gosh, how has he managed that?
Rick: He sleeps at night!

. . .

Molly: Why do you wear your wedding ring on the wrong finger?
Polly: I married the wrong man.

. . .

Customer: I'd like a pair of alligator shoes, please.
Shoe shop manager: Certainly, madam, what size does your alligator take?

STUPID JOKES FOR KIDS

Selections from
**THE GREAT BIG FAT
GIANT JOKE BOOK**

BALLANTINE BOOKS • NEW YORK

A Ballantine Book
Published by The Random House Publishing Group

Published in the United States by Ballantine Books, an imprint of The Random House Publishing Group, a division of Random House, Inc., New York, and simultaneously in Canada by Random House of Canada Limited, Toronto.

This work consists of portions of *The Great Big Fat Giant Joke Book* originally published by Cliveden Press in Great Britain in 1989.

www.ballantinebooks.com

ISBN 0-345-37062-7

This edition published by arrangement with World International Publishing Limited

First Ballantine Books Edition: February 1991

OPM   21   20   19   18   17   16   15

What do you call a cat who has swallowed a duck?
  A duck-filled-fatty puss.

Where do cats like to go on vacation?
  The Canary Islands.

What did the cowboy say when his dog left?
  Doggone.

What do you get when you cross jelly with a sheep-dog?
  Collie-wobbles.

Doctor, doctor, everyone keeps being rude to me.
  Clear out of here, will you?

What do you say when an elephant sits on your sofa?

It's time to get a new sofa!

Dick: Every morning I take my dog for a tramp in the fields.
Mick: Does the dog enjoy it?
Dick: Yes, but the tramp's getting rather fed up.

Did you hear about the man who ate soapflakes for breakfast?

He was so mad he foamed at the mouth and was all in a lather.

Teacher: What is the difference between lightning and electricity?
Pupil: You don't have to pay for lightning.

Daffy definition:
What is the definition of a caterpillar?
A worm wearing a striped sweater.

What do you get when you cross a bee with a bell?

A real humdinger.

Why did the orange stop in the middle of the expressway?

It ran out of juice.

A skinflint needed a hearing aid, but wasn't prepared to pay for one, so he just hung a piece of string beside his ear.

"But can you hear any better?" a friend asked.

"No," the man replied, "but everyone shouts at me now."

Ed: Where did you buy that lovely Easter tie?
Ted: Why do you call it an Easter tie?
Ed: It's got egg on it.

Chef (to complaining customer): But I put my heart and soul into that beef casserole.
Complaining customer: I wish you'd put some beef in, too.

Teacher: Today we're going to talk about pine trees. Which pine has the longest needles?
Billy: I know, sir—the porcu-pine!

Which monkeys like eating lemon pie?

Meringue-outans!

3

Farmer Brown: I've just bought a piece of land ten miles long and an inch wide.
Farmer Giles: What are you going to grow on it?
Farmer Brown: Spaghetti!

Dentist: Would you mind making a few screaming noises, Mr. Nelland? The waiting room is full of patients and I want to leave early for a game of golf.

Knock, knock.
Who's there?
Arthur.
Arthur who?
Arthur any jobs available?

Lady at zoo: Oh look, aren't those tiny lion cubs sweet? I wonder what they'd say if they could talk?
Zookeeper: I think they'd probably say, "We're tigers, not lions!"

Why did the elephant walk on two legs?
   To give the ants a chance.

I'll have to fire my chauffeur—he's nearly killed me twice.
   Don't be too hard on him. Give him one more chance.

Old judge: It would appear that the defendant is not telling the truth.
Defendant: Why's that, sir?
Old judge: Well, you told the court that you have only one brother, but your sister says that she has two brothers . . .

Teacher: Mike, can you give me a sentence using the word "miniature"?
Mike: You start snoring the miniature asleep.

Why does a lion kneel before it springs?
   Because it is preying.

What do you call a cat that sucks lemons?
   A sour puss.

Knock, knock.
Who's there?
Alison.
Alison who?
Alison Wonderland.

Teacher: What's a Grecian urn?
Pupil: About $100 a week.

What kind of tie does a pig wear?
  A pigsty.

Why is tennis such a noisy game?
  Because each player raises a racket.

Mother Owl: I'm worried about our boy.
Father Owl: Why?
Mother Owl: He just doesn't seem to give a hoot about anything.

A pair of goats found a reel of movie film, and began to chomp away at it, each starting at one end. When they met in the middle one goat said: "This is good, isn't it?" The other goat replied: "Its OK, but I preferred the book."

1st Cowboy: Did you find that horse well behaved?
2nd Cowboy: Sure did. When he came to a fence he let me go over first.

Two caterpillars were resting on a leaf one summer's day, when a butterfly flew overhead. "You'll never get me up in one of those!" said one.

Doctor: Have you ever had this before?
Patient: Yes.
Doctor: Well, you've got it again.

Jane: Have you changed the water in the goldfish bowl?
Jean: No, it hasn't drunk what I gave it yesterday yet.

What kind of umbrella does the president have on a rainy day?
A wet one.

I'm trying.
Yes, you're very trying.

What happens after a dry spell?
It rains.

Who always whistles while he works?
A traffic policeman.

How high do people usually stand?
  Over two feet.

What would you call two banana skins?
  A pair of slippers.

What's the difference between a hill and a pill?
  A hill is hard to get up and a pill is hard to get
  down.

My grandfather had a wooden leg.
  That's nothing—mine had a pine chest.

*What do you get when you cross saltines with a
duck?*
  Quackers.

What goes, "Kcauq, kcauq"?
  A duck flying backwards.

What is JR's favorite sweet?
  Ewing gum.

What language do ducks speak?
  Double Ducks.

Singer: Did you notice how my voice filled the whole room tonight?
Friend: Yes, a lot of people had to leave to make room for it.

Teacher: Can you tell me something important that did not exist one hundred years ago?
Polly: Yes—me.

Doctor, doctor, I feel like a vegetable.
  Sit down and lettuce take a look at you.

Doug: What are you making with your chemistry set?
Dave: A liquid that will dissolve anything at all.
Doug: That's great! What will you keep it in?

Boss: I'm sorry, I can't give you a job. I just haven't got enough work to keep you busy.
Boy: I think you'd be surprised at how little it takes to keep me busy.

9

Doctor, doctor, I feel like a snail.
  You'll be all right when you come out of your shell.

Where do tadpoles go to change into frogs?
  Into the croakroom.

Did you hear about the boy who was called 7¼?
  His father pulled his name out of a hat.

What does Kojak write with?
  A baldpoint pen.

Knock, knock.
Who's there?
Aba.
Aba who?
A banana.

Knock, knock.
Who's there?
Ivor.
Ivor who?
Ivor sore hand from knocking on this door.

How can you close an envelope under water?
  With a seal.

What's the definition of an optimist?
  A man who falls from the top of the Eiffel Tower and says on the way down, "Well, I'm not hurt yet."

I once stayed at an old hotel that was so quiet that the ghosts jumped out in the middle of the night yelling, "What was that noise?"

Did you hear about the thief who stole a calendar?
  He got twelve months.

What happened at the flea circus?
  A dog came on and stole the show.

Dad: What did you learn at school today, son?
Son: I learned that all those math examples you did for me were wrong.

Did you hear what happened when the cannibals ate the whole team of football players?
  They had to warm up the substitute.

What country is useful at meal times?
  China.

Why did Dracula take medicine?
  To stop his coffin.

What did the tie say to the hat?
  You go on a head and I'll hang around.

What is black, white and very difficult?
  An exam paper.

What do you call someone who breaks into a butcher's shop?
  A hamburglar.

12

Teacher: Alison, make a sentence using the word "satellite."

Alison: On July Fourth we bought a big firecracker and satellite to it!

Eileen: An apple comes under fruit, a cauliflower comes under vegetables, so what does an egg come under?

Helen: A hen, what else?

Teacher: Benjamin, what period follows the Bronze Age?

Benjamin: The Silver Age, and if we're really lucky, the Gold Age!

What keeps the moon in place?
  Its beams.

What is the difference between an angry rabbit and a counterfeit $10 bill?
  One's a mad bunny and the other's bad money.

Policeman: When I saw you driving down the road I thought to myself "Fifty-five at least."

Motorist: Well, that's not quite fair. I think this hat makes me look older.

13

Boss: Did you put those circulars in the mail?
Secretary: No, sir. I couldn't find any round envelopes for them.

Peter: That's a funny pair of socks you've got on. One sock's blue and the other's yellow.
Paul: Yes, I noticed that. And the funny thing is, I've got another pair at home exactly the same.

Ann: Did you hear the one about the rope?
Jan: No.
Ann: Oh, skip it.

A man was waiting to make a speech, and he was so nervous that he went to a quiet place and started pacing up and down. "Are you very nervous?" a voice asked him. "No, not at all!" insisted the man. "Then what are you doing here in the Ladies Room?"

Customer: I asked for a dozen eggs, and you only sent eleven.
Grocer: That's right—one was cracked so I didn't bother putting it in the box.

Mother: Why did you put this toad in your sister's bed?

Little boy: I couldn't find a mouse.

Hotel guest: Does the water always come through the ceiling like this?

Desk clerk: Oh no, sir; only when it rains.

Interviewer: But aren't you the same boy who came here last week after the same job?

Applicant: Yes sir.

Interviewer: And didn't I tell you that I wanted an older boy?

Applicant: Yes sir. That's why I've come back. I am older now.

Reporter: What makes you so sure the Moon is uninhabited?

Astronaut: Well, when we started to dig a hole, no one came to watch.

Boy: I wish I'd lived in the old days.

Teacher: Why?

Boy: Because then there wouldn't have been so much history to learn.

One day a man walked into a McDonald's with two sheepdogs, and he ordered three hamburgers. The manager was somewhat surprised, but all three of them ate their meals with such obvious enjoyment that he couldn't help but smile. The next day the same man walked in with three Persian cats, and again, all enjoyed their meals. "I can see you're an animal lover," said the manager on the third day, when the man came in with a pet lobster. "That's right," said the man. "And as a matter of fact I wanted to thank you for serving us so kindly these past couple of days. Some people don't like serving my pets. To show my appreciation, I've brought you this lobster. He's yours to keep." "Oh thank you," said the manager, gingerly accepting the live lobster. "He certainly is a beauty. I'll take him home and my wife and I will have him for dinner." "Well," said the animal lover, "he's already had his dinner, but I think he'd enjoy going to the movies."

Teacher: Name six animals of the polar regions.
Pupil: Three walruses and three polar bears.

Why is a baby duckling like an icicle?
   Because they both grow down.

Teacher: Why do we say Amen after prayer, and not Awomen?
Duffy: Because we sing hymns, not hers . . .

How can you avoid falling hair?
   Get out of the way fast!

Why did the young ghoul measure himself against the wall?
   Because he wanted to know if he'd gruesome.

Why were the Middle Ages also called the Dark Ages?
   Because there were lots of knights in those days, sir.

What do liars do when they die?
   Lie still.

Mother: How many times must I tell you to close your eyes during prayers, John?
John: How do you know I don't, Mother . . . ?

What is yellow, and sails the seas observing marine life?
   Jacques Custard.

A rich Texan walked into a car showroom. "My wife has a bad cold," he told the salesman. "What do you have in the way of get-well-soon cars?"

Sam: I've just discovered oil.
Sally: Great—let's go out and buy a new car.
Sam: No, I think we'll get the old one fixed—that's where the oil's coming from.

Guidance counselor: What are you going to do when you grow up?
Boy: I'm going to follow my father's footsteps and be a policeman.
Guidance counselor: Oh, so your father's a policeman?
Boy: No, he's a burglar.

For how long did Cain dislike his brother?
  For as long as he was Abel.

What goes tick tock woof, tick tock woof?
  A watch dog.

What goes tick tock croak, tick tock croak?
   A watch frog.

When can you go as fast as a race car?
   When you're inside it.

If you feed a cow on hundred dollar bills what will you get?
   Rich milk.

Darren: My neighbors are always banging on the wall.
Warren: Does it keep you awake?
Darren: No, but it does interfere with drum practice.

"Who shall I ask for?" the customer said.
   "My name is Crusoe, sir."
   "Oh, really. May I ask what your first name is?"
   "Robinson, sir."
   "Indeed? That is a well-known name."
   "Well, it ought to be, I've been here for the past twenty years."

19

Artist: I can paint a picture in five days and think nothing of it.
Buyer: And neither does anyone else.

Cannibal: You can't boil him, he's a friar.

"That's a marvelous stuffed lion you've got."
  "Yes, I call it Henry."
  "Why?"
  "After my uncle."
  "Why, did he catch it?"
  "No, I caught it, but it had eaten him first."

Teacher: Why did you say that Robinson Crusoe was a contortionist?
Pupil: Because it says when he was shipwrecked, he sat on his chest.

Smith: I hate paying my tax bill.
Brown: You should pay up with a smile.
Smith: I've offered them a smile, but they insist on money.

Smith: How long can a person live without a brain?
Jones: How old are you?

What do you call a man who sits on an easel?
  Art.

What did the impatient stag say to his daughter?
  Hurry up, deer.

Father: How are you getting on in your new job, son?
Son: Great. The boss says I've got everything so mixed up that he can't do without me.

Husband: I'm home, Freda, you can serve the salad.
Freda: How did you know we were having salad?
Husband: There's no smell of burning.

Our school lunches are so cold, even the potatoes keep their jackets on!

Husband: I've cooked some steak that will melt in your mouth.
Wife: Do you mean you haven't defrosted it?

Why don't robots panic?
  Because they have nerves of steel.

21

Customer: That's the hat I want. The one with the red cherries, the green grapes, and the pink peach.
Assistant: Certainly, madam. Shall I put it in a box?
Customer: No, I'll eat it now.

Why do elephants have trunks?
  Because they have no pockets to put things in.

What never asks questions but gets pressed for answers?
  A doorbell.

Knock, knock.
Who's there?
Lettuce.
Lettuce who?
Lettuce in and you'll soon find out!

Why couldn't the boy open the piano lock?
  Because all the keys were inside.

How do we know the ocean is friendly?
  Because it waves.

What's worse than a crocodile with a toothache?
  A centipede with sore feet.

What zooms along under the sea on three wheels?
  A motor-pike and side-carp.

Father: Thomas, please keep quiet. I'm trying to read.
Thomas: What? I learned how years ago!

How can you carry water in a sieve?
  Make it into a block of ice first.

Cannibal husband: How many people for dinner tonight?
Cannibal wife: Two each.

What can be right but never wrong?
  An angle.

Wife: My husband thinks he's a TV antenna.
Doctor: I think I can cure him.
Wife: I don't want him cured, just adjusted. I can't get channel 4.

Did you hear about the girl who did bird impressions?

She ate worms for breakfast.

Knock, knock.
Who's there?
Noah.
Noah who?
Noah fence, but we're full up.

An old lady was in an old rickety elevator. "If we break down, will I go up or down?" she asked the attendant.

The attendant smiled. "That depends on the kind of life you've been leading," he replied.

Teacher: If I had six apples and wanted to divide them among eight children, how would I do it?
Pupil: Make a pie.

Billy: I got the highest grade in math. The teacher asked what twelve times twelve is, and I said one hundred and ten.
Willy: But that's wrong.
Billy: I know, but I was closer than anyone else in the class.

Dad: You're going to have a new brother or sister soon. Which would you prefer?
Bob: I'd prefer a puppy.

Big Bill isn't really bald, you know, he just has a very tall face.

Policeman: Do you know you were doing ninety miles an hour, son?
New driver: That's great—I only passed my test this morning!

Mom: Remember, never put off till tomorrow what can be done today.
Rob: We'd better eat the rest of the pie, then.

Why is an island like the letter T?
   Because it is in the middle of water.

Sarah: Has anyone lost fifty cents?
Sue: I have.
Sara: Where did you lose it?
Sue: Where you found it.

Will February March? No, but April May before
June.

Sam: I know everything there is to know about
tennis.
Pam: OK—how many holes are there in a tennis
net?

What's the best way to get in touch with a shark?
   Drop him a line.

What do you call a sheep that's just been sheared?
   Bare, bare, black sheep.

What travels underground at 80 miles an hour?
   A mole on a motorbike.

Dad, do you like baked apples?
   Yes, son, why?
   The orchard's on fire.

What's the worst trip to take? A long sea voyage? A transatlantic flight?
  No—the trip to the principal's office.

What do people sing in their baths?
  Soap operas.

What's the cheapest way to see the world?
  Buy an atlas.

Teacher: Boys, boys, you mustn't fight like that, you should learn to give and take.
1st boy: I did—I gave him a whack and took his apple . . .

Boss: Miss Smith, why is there a gherkin behind your ear?
Secretary: Oh dear, I must have eaten my pencil.

What goes "ha, ha, ha, plop!"?
  Someone laughing his head off.

What should you do if you see a great big tiger?
  Hope that the tiger doesn't see little old you.

27

Teacher: What does plural mean?
Boy: The same, only more of it.

Little girl: Mommy, why are your hands so soft?
Mother: Because I always use new Suddso on my dishes.
Little girl: But why does that make your hands soft?
Mother: Because the money the Suddso people pay me for this commercial has bought me an automatic dishwasher.

Teacher: Johnny, when am I going to see an improvement in your work?
Johnny: When you put your glasses on!

Joanne: Which part of going to school do you like best?
Penny: The holidays.

What do you call a disastrous cat?
A catastrophe!

What did the mother raspberry say to the baby raspberry?
Now son, make sure you don't get into a jam.

28

What did the horse say when he got to the bottom of his nose bag?

That's the last straw!

An old lady was in a pet shop. "I want to buy a collar for my dog," she said.

"How big is the dog?" asked the shopkeeper.

The old lady held her hands apart. "About this big," she said.

"Why don't you bring your dog in so that we can measure him properly," the shopkeeper suggested.

"Oh, I couldn't do that," said the old lady. "It's going to be a surprise for him."

Customer: Waiter, this fish is bad.
Waiter: You naughty fish, you!

Hunter: I heard the lion roaring in the night, so I jumped out of bed and shot him in my nightshirt.
Friend: What was a lion doing in your nightshirt?

I have six eyes, two mouths and three ears. What am I?

Ugly.

Why were the postman and the chimney sweep in court?

They were accused of blackmail.

What does the winner of a race lose?
  His breath.

What wears shoes but has no feet?
  The pavement.

Where would you find flying rabbits?
  In the hare force.

What's the easiest way to widen a road?
  Just add a B and it becomes broad right away.

Passenger: Doñ't drive so fast. You frighten me taking curves like that!
Driver: Just close your eyes, like I do . . .

What happened to the man who took his dog for a walk along the gutter?
  He fell off the roof!

My brother is very superstitious. He won't work any week that has a Friday in it.

What's the definition of radio?
  Television without the pictures.

Did you her about the tailor who bought a cheap batch of windowshade material?
  He made it up into trousers, but every time the sun went down, the trouser legs rolled up.

Customer: I want to buy a good revolver.
Gunsmith: How about a six-shooter?
Customer: Can you make it a nine-shooter? It's for the cat next door.

What do you call a man with a seagull on his head?
  Cliff.

What can you break without touching?
  Your promise.

Fortune-teller: I see great disappointment for someone close to you.
Customer: That's right—I've no money to pay you.

Which is the saddest tree?
   The weeping willow.

Why are bad friends like the pages of an old book?
   They keep falling out.

Why should you always wear a watch in the desert?
   Because they have springs in them.

Bill: What does illegal mean?
Bob: A sick bird.

Customer: I want to sit on my wife's right hand.
Waiter: Wouldn't you be more comfortable on a chair?

Did you hear about the old lady who told knitting jokes?
   She was a real nit wit.

Stranger: What's the quickest way to the town hall?
Boy: Run as fast as you can.

Mom: Eat your dinner, Eric.
Eric: I'm waiting for the mustard to cool down.

Why are the letters O and N important?
  Because we can't get ON without them.

Joe: Do squirrels bark?
Flo: No.
Joe: But it says in this book that squirrels eat acorns and bark.

Jimmy: What sort of animal would you most like to be?
Johnny: A duck.
Jimmy: Why?
Johnny: Because I've never been one.

Ed: What is a gentleman farmer?
Ned: A man who milks cows wearing a top hat.
Ed: I've never seen cows wearing top hats.

Teacher: Name a collective noun.
Pupil: Wastebasket.

What are the largest ants in the world?
  Giants.

Mr. Smith: I'm worried, Martha. Jim's taken some money from my wallet again.
Mrs. Smith: How do you know it was Jim? I could have taken it.
Mr. Smith: No you couldn't—there's $5 left . . .

What do you write on a robot's gravestone?
  Rust in piece.

What do you call a sleeping light bulb?
  A bulbdozer.

Why will the world never come to an end?
  Because it is round.

Patient: I keep thinking I'm a bridge.
Doctor: What's come over you?
Patient: Oh, a truck, two buses, five cars . . .

Mr. Snitch: That Mrs. Green who lives down the road often takes her husband away for the weekend. Why don't you do that?
Mrs. Snitch: I don't like him.

Tramp: Please, can you spare me a piece of layer cake?
Lady: Won't a piece of bread and butter do?
Tramp: Not today, lady—it's my birthday.

How do Arabs like to dance?
  Sheik to Sheik!

What's the difference between a friend and a fiend?
  The letter "r"!

Joe: If I were a river, I'd have a lot of money.
Jim: Why do you think that?
Joe: Because I'd run between two banks!

When can't you eat an orange?
  When it's a drink!

What happens to an old suit when you throw it in a river?
   It changes into a wet suit!

What demands an answer without asking a question?
   A telephone!

Rick: My Dad hasn't slept for twelve days, but he isn't a bit tired.
Dick: Gosh, how has he managed that?
Rick: He sleeps at night!

When is a child not its father's son?
   When it's his daughter!

What sort of table can you not sit at?
   A timetable!

Mac: Our dog is just like one of the family, you know.
Jack: Which one—your grandad?

36

What did one daisy say to the other daisy?
   Take me to your weeder.

What do you get if you cross a chicken with a clock?
   Chick tock, chick tock, chick tock.

Teacher: I'm now going to tell you all about the elephant, but if you don't pay attention and look at me, you won't know what it looks like . . .

Knock, knock.
Who's there?
Beezer.
Beezer who?
Beezer black and yellow.

Jim: Mum, there's a big black cat in the kitchen.
Mom: That's all right, black cats are lucky.
Jim: This one is—he's eaten the roast.

Knock, knock.
Who's there?
Snow.
Snow who?
Snow use, I've forgotten the name.

Waitress: There you are, madam, a sundae with vanilla ice cream, strawberry ice cream, maple syrup, chocolate sauce, fresh peach slices, whipped cream, chocolate chips and nuts. Would you like a cherry?
Customer: No thanks—I'm on a diet.

Who invented fireplaces?
   Alfred the Grate.

Knock, knock.
Who's there?
Norma Lee.
Norma Lee who?
Norma Lee we go swimming on Sundays, but I thought we'd see you instead.

What did the car say to the road?
   You're round the bend.

Have you ever seen a catfish?
   How did it hold the rod?

When is it correct to say "I is"?
   When the letter I is the next letter in the alphabet after "H."

When are you guaranteed to find the needle you dropped?
   When you have nothing on your feet.

What has a neck but no head?
   A bottle of lemonade.

What did the dog say to the flea?
   You bug me!

What are white and furry and ride horses?
   Polo bears.

What is yours, but used by others all the time?
   Your name.

Judge: You are accused of having stolen a turkey. What have you to say?
Man: I took it for a lark.
Judge: A turkey looks nothing like a lark. Fined ten dollars!

What can you make that no one can see?
  A noise.

Tim: What kind of robber is a page, Dad?
Dad: What do you mean?
Tim: It says in the paper, "Two pages held up the bride's train."

There was a young man from Leeds,
Who swallowed a packet of seeds,
In a month, oh alas,
He was covered in grass,
And he even had one or two weeds.

How do you make a frankfurter roll?
  Push it.

Sam: Mom, can I have another apple?
Mom: Another apple? They don't grow on trees, you know!

What swings around a candy shop?
  Tarzipan.

When you take away two letters from this five-letter word you are left with one. What's the word?
  Stone.

What do you call a lazy dinosaur?
  A stegosnaurus.

What did the two big chimneys say to the little chimney?
  You're too young to smoke.

Teacher: This essay on your pet cat is word for word the same as your brother's.
Mark: It's the same cat.

Don't worry if your job is small,
And your rewards are few.
Remember that the mighty oak,
Was once a nut like you.

Teacher: What is meant by dogma?
Girl: A mother of pups.

Landlady: Full board will be twenty dollars for the week.
Boxer: How about for the strong?

The small boy was very clever. In a quiz, the teacher asked him how he had gained so much knowledge. "Well," said the boy, "I picked up a bit here and a bit there, and I was too lazy to forget it."

Fred: What a lovely brown cow. It's a jersey, isn't it?
Ed: Is it? I thought it was its skin . . .

Lady on bus: I'm afraid I haven't anything less than this $5 bill.
Driver: Is that all you have?
Lady: Oh, no, I've got $50 in the bank, too.

Boss: I'm a man of few words, son. When I beckon with my finger, it means I want you.
New boy: And when I shake my head, it means I'm not coming.

Who lives in Australia?
   Sydney.

A boss was talking about her assistant. "He's like a blotter," she said. "He soaks up everything I say, but gets it all backwards."

A girl was about to go into the sea. "Aren't you afraid of sharks?" said her friend.

"No," the girl replied. "They're man-eating sharks."

Why is the letter G like the sun?
Because it is the center of light.

What is it that you cannot hold for fifteen minutes, even though it is lighter than a feather?
Your breath.

Why do you go up to bed?
Because the bed won't come down to you.

If you were locked out of your house, how would you get in?
Sing and sing until you find the right key.

What always ends everything?
  The letter G.

What flower does everyone have?
  Tulips.

Why did the comedian tell jokes in front of a mirror?
  He wanted to see it crack up.

What is easy to get into—but hard to get out of?
  Trouble.

If a green stone fell into the Red Sea what would happen?
  It would sink.

Teacher: Name five members of the cat family.
Pupil: Mother cat, father cat, and three kittens.

Why was Cinderella such a poor runner?
  Because she had a pumpkin for a coach.

What is all over the house?
  The roof.

Daffy definitions:
Jack-in-the box: an open and shut case.
Library: a tall building with lots of stories.

Why are fish so smart?
  Because they go around in schools.

Molly: Why do you wear your wedding ring on the wrong finger?
Polly: I married the wrong man.

Why is your nose in the middle of your face?
  Because it's the center.

What do you get if you cross a shark with a parrot?
  An animal that talks your head off.

A young actor got his first part and rushed off to tell his father the news. "I play a man who's been married for twenty years," he said.
  "Never mind, son," said his father. "Perhaps you'll get a speaking part next."

Knock knock.
Who's there?
Wendy.
Wendy who?
Wendy joke is over you had better laugh.

Ned: Did you hear about the stupid girl who goes around saying no all the time?
Sally: No.
Ned: Oh, it's you, is it?

What game do spacemen play?
  Moonopoly.

What fish would you serve with peanut butter?
  A jellyfish.

How do Indians send secret messages?
  With smokeless fuel.

Why is the letter V like an angry bull?
  Because it comes after "U."

What is in the middle of Paris?
  The letter R.

What cheese is made backwards?
  Edam.

Referee: That was a late tackle.
Football Player: But I got there as soon as I could . . .

Woman: Are you the boy who just saved my son from drowning?
Young man: Yes, it was me.
Woman: Well, would you mind going in again for his cap?

Mrs. Brown arrived at her son's front door with her suitcase in her hand. "Do you mind if I stay here for a few days?" she asked.
  "Not at all," said her son. "If there's anything you want, just knock."

Teacher: How many days of the week begin with the letter T?
Pupil: Four—Tuesday, Thursday, Today, and To-morrow.

Which fish live in heaven?
  Angelfish.

Doctor, doctor, I feel like a pair of scissors.
  Now you can just cut that out . . .

What do you get if you cross a rabbit with a spider?
  A hairnet.

What would Neptune say if all the seas dried up?
  I haven't a notion.

Ken: I see that film actress Sasa Grabmore has
been voted Housekeeper of the Year again by the
newspapers.
Len: Is that right?
Ken: Yes, every time she gets a divorce she keeps
the house . . .

What's the definition of a sculptor?
  A chip off the old block.

What did the boy candle say to the girl candle?
   Will you go out with me?

Teacher: Your hair's a disgrace. Have you combed it?
Boy: No.
Teacher: What would you say if I came into school looking like that?
Boy: I'd be far too polite to mention it.

Knock, knock.
Who's there?
Scot.
Scot who?
Scot nothing to do with you!

Knock, knock.
Who's there?
Sacha.
Sacha who?
Sacha fuss, just because I knocked at your door.

What happened to the cat who swallowed a ball of yarn?
   She had mittens.

"Excuse me, can you tell me the time?"
  "I'm sorry, I'm a stranger here myself."

Father: At your age, son, I could name all the kings and queens of England.
Son: Yes, but there were only three or four of them then.

Who earns a living by driving his customers away?
  A taxi driver.

Pupil: I didn't deserve a zero on this paper!
Teacher: No, but there weren't any lower marks.

What did one eye say to the other eye?
  Just between us something smells.

What did you buy your brother for his birthday?
  A spaceship.
  Was he happy?
  Happy? He was over the moon!

Doctor, doctor, I feel like an apple.
  Sit down, Mr. Smith, I won't eat you.

How much is that skunk worth?
    A cent.

Teacher: John, how many seasons are there in a year?
John: Two—baseball and football.

What job do hippies do?
    They hold your leggies on.

The elephant looked down at the little mouse and commented, "My, my, aren't you little."
    The mouse was very offended. "Well, I've been ill," he said.

Malcolm used to go out with a printer's daughter, but it turned out that he wasn't really her type.

All our furniture goes back to Louis the fourteenth—if we don't pay Louis for it before the fourteenth, that is.

I always follow the same routine, you know. I get up at seven, every morning, no matter what time it is . . .

Mother: Why don't you yawn when Dave stays too long—he'll take the hint and go, I'm sure.
Daughter: I tried that—he just said what amazing tonsils I had.

What sporting event did the kangaroo, the little girl and the frog enter?
    The hop, skip and jump.

Eskimo Bill: Where does your mom come from?
Eskimo Bob: Alaska.
Eskimo Bill: Don't bother—I'll ask her myself.

What do confused chickens lay?
    Scrambled eggs!

What did the first tonsil say to the second tonsil?
    Get dressed quickly—the doctor's taking us out!

Did you hear about the witch who was top of the class?

Yes—she was the best speller.

Jill: I've just bought a great new wig. Do you think I should tell Jim about it?

Jack: No, I'd keep it under my hat if I were you.

Where does a chimney sweep keep his brushes?

In a soot case.

Lady cannibal: I just don't know what to make of my husband these days!

Friend: How about croquettes?

What would the duckling say if it saw an orange in its nest?

Look at the orange marmalade (mama laid)!

Man in elevator: Sixth floor, please.

Elevator man: Here you are, son.

Man in elevator: How dare you call me son!

Elevator man: Well, I brought you up, didn't I?

Customer: Have you any cheaper rings than this?
Jeweler: Yes sir, but they're stitched to the top of the curtains.

Job hunter: I'm sorry I'm late but I've been up all night with a toothache.
Interviewer: How about a job as a night watchman then?

Which is the fastest, cold or heat?
Heat—because you can catch a cold.

Mom: Danny, did you take a bath this morning?
Dan: Why—is one missing?

Knock, knock.
Who's there?
Robin.
Robin who?
Robin banks.

Mad professor: Did you know that there's a very clever device for looking through brick walls?
Student: Is that so?
Mad professor: Yes, it's called a window.

When is baseball like a crime?
  When it's hit and run.

Man in shop: Can I have two pairs of stockings, please?
Assistant: Certainly, sir. Are they a surprise for your wife?
Man in shop: They certainly are—she's expecting a new coat!

Wife: My clothes are so old and shabby, anyone coming to the house would think I was the cook, not the owner.
Husband: Not if they stayed for dinner they wouldn't.

Teacher: We are only going to have half a day's lessons this morning.
Pupils: Hurrah!
Teacher: Yes, we will have the other half this afternoon . . .

Customer: This shop is a disgrace—I can write my name in the dust on this furniture.
Assistant: It must be wonderful to have an education . . .

Dad: Why do you want to work in a bank?
Son: They say there's money in it.

Doctor, doctor, I keep thinking I'm a comedian.
  You must be joking, Mr. Green.

What do you call an artist who is always grumbling?
  Mona Lisa.

Teacher: Where do pencils come from?
Pupil: Pennsylvania.

What did the big flower say to the little flower?
  Hi, bud.

Man: Why is this station called Fish Hook?
Porter: Because it's at the end of the line.

Sentry: Halt, who goes there?
Recruit: Oh, the name's Smith but you won't know me—I'm new here.

Lodger: My shaving water was dirty this morning.
Landlady: That wasn't shaving water, that was your tea.

Workman: Have you seen this morning's paper?
Apprentice: No, what was in it?
Workman: My lunch.

There was an old woman from Dover
Who decided to knit a pullover.
But would you believe
She knitted four sleeves?
And now it only fits Rover!

Knock, knock.
Who's there?
Fozzie.
Fozzie who?
Fozzie hundredth time, let me in!

Here is a newsflash:

Fifty valuable pedigree dogs have been
stolen from their kennels.
Police say they have no leads.

What did the big tap say to the little tap?
   Shut up, you little squirt.

Why did the Eiffel Tower get its name?
   Because you're sure to get an eyeful from the top.

An ASPCA inspector walked into a fast food shop and spoke to the owner. "I'm here to investigate a complaint that has been made against you," he said. "We've had reports that you've been battering your fish!"

A man walked into the employment agency looking for a job. The only vacancy was for a postman. "Well, I suppose it's better than walking the streets . . ." he said.

Customer: I'd like a pair of alligator shoes, please.
Shoe salesman: Certainly, madam, what size does your alligator take?

When does Friday come before Thursday?
   In the dictionary.

How long was he in the army?
   About six foot seven inches.

What did the hotel manager say to the elephant who, after running up a large bill, couldn't pay?
   "Pack your trunk and go, before I call the police."

A man selling vacuum cleaners appeared at the door of an old lady's cottage and, without allowing the woman to speak, rushed into the living room and threw a large bag of dirt all over her clean carpet. He said, "If this new magical cleaner doesn't pick up every bit of dirt, I'll eat it."
   The woman, who by this time was losing her patience, said, "Sir, if I had enough money to buy that I would have paid my electricity bill before they cut it off. Now, what would you prefer, a spoon or a knife and fork?"

Angela: What do angels do in heaven?
Minister: They play the harp and sing.
Angela: Haven't they ever heard of radios?

Director: The show must go on.
Critic: Yes, but in this case, why?

What makes it hard to talk when a goat is around?
  He always butts in.

Knock, knock.
Who's there?
Hiram.
Hiram who?
Hiram fine, how are you?

Joe: I've found a job at last, Tony. I'm working down at the dominoes factory putting the spots on the dominoes.
Tony: Why aren't you working today?
Joe: This is the day they made all the double blanks.

Did you hear about the man who jumped off a bridge in Paris?
  He went insane (in Seine).

Which fish is very musical?
  A piano-tuna.

Why are sergeant-majors like dentists?
  They both like drilling.

Why did the potato farmer act high and mighty?
  He had a chip on his shoulder.

Definition of budget: a system of worrying both
before and after you spend money, instead of
just after.

One wise cannibal toasted his mother-in-law for
the wedding dinner.

How do you get down from a rhinoceros?
  You don't, you get down from a duck.

A young soccer player from Lyme
Scored a goal for the very first time.
Although he was glad,
His teammates were sad—
He hadn't changed ends at halftime!

Well, I wouldn't say that Mrs. Jones has a big
mouth, but every time she smiles she gets
lipstick on her ears . . .

What is the difference between a sick elephant and dead bee?

One is a seedy beast and the others is a bee deceased.

I've got five arms, six heads, three eyes and two noses. What am I?

A liar.

Mom: Did you thank Mrs. Green for the lovely birthday party?

Girl: No, Julie thanked her and Mrs. Green said not to mention it—so I didn't.

What do you get if you cross a big dog with a telephone?

A golden receiver.

How do you stop your feet falling asleep?

Wear loud socks.

Have you heard about the man with five legs?

His trousers fit him like a glove.

Husband: What do you mean, there's no dinner because of a power cut? We have a gas stove!
Wife: I know, but the can opener's electric.

Why did the bald man stick his head out of the train window?
   To get some fresh air (hair).

Doctor, doctor, I feel like a telephone.
   Go home, Mr. Smith, and ring me later.

What zips down the clothesline at 30 miles per hour?
   Hondapants.

What is the definition of an undercover agent?
   A spy in bed.

What escaped when the house burned down?
   The door bolted.

What else escaped when the house burned down?
   The chimney flew.

What else escaped when the house burned down?
  The tap ran.

Shopkeeper: What can I get for you?
Customer: I'd like a mousetrap. Hurry, please—I've got a bus to catch.
Shopkeeper: I'm sorry, we don't have any that big.

What is the brightest day of the week?
  Sunday.

A man was taking his first golf lesson and he wasn't doing very well. "I'd move heaven and earth to hit a good shot," he said to the golf coach.
  "Concentrate on heaven," said the golf coach. "You've moved enough earth already today."

Teacher: I have three pears, four peaches, six apples and twelve grapes. What have I got?
Pupil: A fruit salad.

Patient: What should I take when I'm run down?
Doctor: The car's license plate.

Diner: I don't like this piece of cod. It's not half as good as the one I ate here two weeks ago.
Waiter: Well it should be—it's from the same fish.

Maid: How do I announce dinner, ma'am? Do I say, "Dinner is ready" or "Dinner is served"?
Mistress: If it's anything like yesterday's meal, just say, "Dinner is ruined!"

There was a young lad from Bombay,
Who never felt happy or gay.
Then he took a good look
At the jokes in this book,
And laughed for the rest of the day.

What nuts remind you of vegetables?
  Peanuts.

What flies yet never goes anywhere?
  A flag.

What pop group kills germs?
  The Bleach Boys.

Where does a sick ship go?
  To the doc's (docks).

The deep-sea diver was swimming along the ocean bed when his support ship sent a message down to him. "Come up immediately," the message read. "We're sinking!"

Doctor, doctor, people keep ignoring me.
  Next!

What do ghosts like to ride on in an amusement park?
  The roller ghoster.

What happened to the man who stole ten bars of soap?
  He made a clean getaway.

Boss: Why are you so late?
Worker: I overslept.
Boss: You mean you sleep at home, too?

Job advertisement seen in the paper:
MAN WANTED TO MAKE BATTERIES—MUST
BE ABLE TO TAKE CHARGE.

What can you serve, but never eat?
A tennis ball.

What turns without moving?
Milk—when it turns sour.

What did the bird say to the scarecrow?
I'll knock the stuffing out of you.

*What happened to the plastic surgeon when he
warmed his hands in front of the fire?*
He melted.

One of my uncles was a doctor, but he gave it
all up. He just didn't have the patients.

Knock, knock.
Who's there?
Dishwasher.
Dishwasher who?
Dishwashn't the way I shpoke before I had false teeth.

Look, I've got a new pack of jumbo-sized cards.
  Big deal!

What do you get if you cross a cocoa bean with Bullwinkle?
  A chocolate moose.

What do you get if you cross a sheep with a rain storm?
  A wet blanket.

What is the healthiest kind of water?
  Well water.

What happened when the cat drank fifty saucers of milk?
  It created a lap record.

What did the bull say when he had visited the china shop?
   I've had a smashing time.

Knock, knock.
Who's there?
Darwin.
Darwin who?
I'll be Darwin you open the door.

What is the perfect cure for dandruff?
   Baldness.

Why is a baker an unselfish person?
   Because he is continually selling that which he kneads himself.

Which bird is always out of breath?
   A puffin.

Knock, knock.
Who's there?
Eva.
Eva who?
Eva you're deaf or your door bell isn't working.

Patient: Will my chicken pox be better next week, Doctor?

Doctor: I don't know, I hate to make rash promises.

Why are ghosts such good actors?
  There are so many phantomimes.

What do they call the noise made by the crowd at Wimbledon?
  A tennis racket.

Knock, knock.
Who's there?
You.
You who?
Did you call me?

Jim: Dad, can I have fifty cents to give to a little old lady?

Dad: Where is she?

Jim: Behind the counter in the candy shop.

Man in line: Hey, who do you think you're pushing?

Other man: I don't know—what's your name?

How do you keep flies out of the kitchen?
   Keep your garbage can in the living room.

Unhappy wife: Did you notice that, Kathleen? As soon as Bill went out into the garden, the birds stopped singing.

What does Pinocchio say when he's got a cold?
   Shiver me timbers.

Where does a sheep go for a haircut?
   A baa-baa shop.

Where do you leave your dog when you go shopping?
   In a barking lot.

What happened when the frog's car broke down on the highway?
   He was toad away.

How does a ship hear things?
   Through its engineers.

What do bees sing when it's raining?
  I'm stinging in the rain, just stinging in the rain . . .

A little girl went to the zoo with her mother. She stared and stared at the zebras until her mother asked her what was wrong. "It's those horses," the little girl said. "It's nearly suppertime and they've still got their pajamas on."

What is hot all year round?
  Mustard.

Jim: Hi, Mom, is dinner ready? I'm starving.
Jim's mother: No, dinner's only half cooked.
Jim: That's all right—I'll eat the half that's cooked and leave the rest till later.

What table is made of paper and has no legs?
  A timetable.

Amateur boxer: Did I do any damage?
Coach: No, but keep swinging your fists and the draft you create might give him a cold.

Mother: What did you learn in cooking class today?
Daughter: We haven't got as far as cooking yet—we've only done thawing.

Did you hear about the composer who only worked in bed? He composed sheet music.

Daffy definition:
A cannibal is a person who walks into a restaurant and orders a waiter.

Did you hear about the wealthy heiress? She has four cars—one for driving in each direction.

What's your favorite dish?
   A clean one.

Sue: Why are you reading that travel book backwards?
Pru: I'm on the return journey.

Patient: What's good for long nails?
Doctor: Sharp teeth.

A man was sprinkling white powder on his front garden.

"What's the powder for?" asked his neighbor.

"It's to keep the elephants off the grass," replied the first man.

"But we don't get any elephants around here!"

"I know—great stuff, isn't it?"

What is red, gray, red, gray, red, gray?
A striped tie rolling down a hill.

What do cats read every morning?
Mewspapers.

Why does the apple tree cry a lot?
Because people are always picking on him.

Why do bats hang upside down?
So they can drop off to sleep.

What kind of robbery is least dangerous?
   A safe robbery.

Teacher: Jerry, can you name a shooting star?
Jerry: Clint Eastwood.

Sergeant: I want you to be on the lookout for this man. He's wearing a paper suit, a paper hat, and he's carrying a paper bag.
Policeman: What's he wanted for?
Sergeant: Rustling.

Knock, knock.
Who's there?
Atlas.
Atlas who?
Atlas it's Friday.

What is an octopus?
   A cat with eight heads.

What is a centimeter?
   A meter with one hundred legs.

When is a pie like a poet?
  When it's Browning.

When is a boxer like a postage stamp?
  When he's licked and put in a corner.

What did the chimney sweep say about his job?
  It soots me fine.

What kind of criminal is the strongest?
  A shoplifter.

How does a flea get from one place to another?
  By itch-hiking.

There was an old woman from Ealing
Who went for a walk on the ceiling.
She murmured, "By heck!"
As she fell on her neck.
"That was a curious feeling!"

Why did your grandma put wheels on her rocking chair?
She wanted to rock and roll.

What can you put into a glass bottle, but never take out?
A crack.

Why did the match box?
Because it saw the ski jump.

Why did the fruit punch?
Because it saw the wood fence.

Why did the spy spray his room with insect repellent?
Because he thought it was bugged.

What do you get when you cross a dog with an elephant?
A very nervous postman.

What do ghouls eat for breakfast?
  Dreaded Wheat.

What's a rabbit's favorite candy?
  A lollihop.

Molly: What nationality are you?
Polly: Well, my father was born in Iceland and my mother was born in Cuba.
Molly: Oh, so you're an Ice Cube?

Customer: I didn't come here to be insulted.
Assistant: Why, where do you normally go?

Job applicant: Well, do I get the job?
Interviewer: We have one last question which every new employee has to answer. If Captain Cook made five voyages and was killed on one of them, which one was it?
Applicant: Er, couldn't you ask me another question? I'm not very good at history.

Diner: A sirloin steak, please.
Waiter: Would you like anything with it?
Diner: If it's anything like the last one I had here, you'd better bring me a hammer and chisel.

Bruce: Have you any meat for my dog?
Butcher: Only a lamb's foot.
Bruce: He'll like that—he's a sheepdog.

Lawyer: What is the maximum penalty for bigamy?
Judge: Two mothers-in-law.

Why was the tennis ball deaf?
  Because it was subjected to a lot of racket.

Knock, knock.
Who's there?
Boo.
Boo who?
Don't cry—it's only a knock, knock joke.

Where do dogs go when they've lost their tails?
  To a retailer.

Mr. Jones, you've had seven jobs in the past six weeks. Is there any job you think you could stick to?
  Well, I've always wanted to work in a glue factory . . .

What is short, green and likes camping?
   A boy sprout.

What goes 99-thump, 99-thump, 99-thump?
   A centipede with a wooden leg.

Why were the elephants the last animals to leave the ark?
   They had to pack their trunks.

What dog does not bark no matter what you do to him?
   A hot dog.

What cake is as hard as rock?
   Marble cake.

Knock, knock.
Who's there?
Disk.
Disk who?
Disk is a recorded message.

"Waiter!"

"Yes sir?"

"What is this?"

"It's bean soup, sir."

"I don't want to know what it's been, what is it now?"

What kind of leopard has red spots?
A leopard with measles.

What do you get if a bird flies into a lawn mower?
Shredded tweet.

How do you keep a rhinoceros from charging?
Take away his credit cards.

Why do pigs eat so much?
Because they want to make hogs of themselves.

Why are waiters good at multiplication?
Because they know their tables.

Knock, knock.
Who's there?
Dana.
Dana who?
Dana talk with your mouth full.

What did the grape say when the elephant stepped on it?
  It didn't say a word. It just let out a wine.

What sound do two porcupines make when they kiss?
  "Ouch!"

Why did Robin Hood rob the rich?
  Because the poor didn't have any money.

Why did the projector blush?
  It saw a film strip.

How does a snake feel when he sheds his skin?
  Snaked!

What is black when it is clean and white when it is dirty?
   A blackboard.

What is green and can jump a mile a minute?
   A grasshopper with hiccups.

Knock, knock.
Who's there?
Theresa.
Theresa who?
Theresa fly in my soup.

How do you make a Venetian blind?
   Stick a finger in his eye.

What is a stupid flower?
   A blooming idiot.

What kind of car do werewolves buy?
   A Wolfswagen.

Knock, knock.
Who's there?
Howie.
Howie who?
I'm fine, how are you?

How do you cut an ocean in two?
   With a sea-saw.

What do you get if you cross a parrot with a canary?
   A bird that knows both the words and the music.

How do undertakers speak?
   Gravely.

Why do surgeons wear masks during operations?
   Because if they make a mistake, no one will know who did it.

Knock, knock.
Who's there?
Ifor.
Ifor who?
I forgot my key.

When the clock strikes thirteen, what time is it?
   It's time to have the clock fixed.

What kind of music do ghosts like?
   Haunting melodies.

Why did the robot go mad?
   Because he had a screw loose.

Optician: You need glasses.
Customer: How can you tell?
Optician: I knew as soon as you came through the window.

Two astronauts, Jerry and Larry, were orbiting the earth in their spaceship. According to plans, Jerry would leave the spaceship to go on a fifteen-minute space walk while Larry remained inside. When Jerry tried to re-enter the spaceship he found the door was locked. He knocked. No answer. He tried again. There was still no answer. Finally he pounded the door with all his might, and he heard Larry's voice inside the spaceship saying, "Who's there?"

What do you get if you cross an insect and a rabbit?
   Bugs Bunny.

Knock, knock.
Who's there?
Lisa.
Lisa who?
Lisa you can do is let me in.

How did the man feel when he got his electric bill?
   He was shocked.

Customer: Waiter, what's this fly doing in my soup?
Waiter: It looks like the backstroke.

What has four legs, a back and no body?
   A chair.

Why is an acrobat like a whiskey glass?
   Because they are both tumblers.

Teacher: How many feet are there in a yard?
Pupil: Well, it depends on how many people there are.

Knock, knock.
Who's there?
Phyllis.
Phyllis who?
Phyllis in on the news.

What did one fish say to another?
   If you keep your mouth shut you won't get caught.

What colors would you paint the sun and the wind?
   The sun rose and the wind blue.

Was Dracula ever married?
   No, he was a bat-chelor.

What tuba can't you play?
   A tuba toothpaste.

What does a chiropodist like to eat at breakfast time?
   Shredded feet.

What does a cat like to eat at breakfast time?
   Mice crispies.

Why was Robin Hood like a famous artist?
   He was always drawing his bow.

What falls all day yet never gets hurt?
   A waterfall.

Mother: What would you do if your little sister swallowed the door key?
Child: Climb in through the window.

Why do elephants lie in the sun a lot?
   Because no one likes a white elephant.

What do you call a woman with a river on her head?
   Flo.

Boy: Mom, I've just knocked the ladder down.
Mom: Well you'd better tell your father.
Boy: I think he knows already, Mom. He's hanging from the bedroom window.

What does a duck become when it first jumps into water?
   Wet.

What is that selfish girl's name?
   Mimi.

What peels and chips, but never cracks?
   Potatoes.

How long is a shoe?
   One foot long.

First mother: My daughter's at the university. She's very bright, you know. Every time we get a letter from her we have to go to the dictionary.
Second mother: You're lucky—every time we hear from our daughter we have to go to the bank.

What do you give a sick canary?
Tweetment.

What game always has it ups and downs?
Snakes and ladders.

I hear your brother fell into an upholstery machine.
Yes, but he's fully recovered now.

Conductor on train: Don't lean out of the window, son.
Boy: Why not?
Conductor: We don't want any of our bridges damaged.

Bill: Hello, Ben. I'm just calling to ask if you'll lend me $5.
Ben: I can't hear a word you're saying—this is a very bad line.
Operator: I can hear him perfectly.
Ben: You lend him $5 then . . .

Secretary: What silly fool has put these daisies on my desk?
Boss: I did.
Secretary: Oh, aren't they lovely?

A tramp knocked at the door of a bar called George and the Dragon.

"Could you spare a poor man a bit to eat?" he asked the woman who answered the door.

"No!" she screamed, slamming the door.

A few seconds later he knocked again.

"Could I have something to eat please?" said the tramp.

"Go away, you good-for-nothing!" shouted the woman. "And don't come back!"

After a few minutes the tramp knocked for a third time.

The woman came to the door.

"Could I have a few words with George this time?" said the tramp.

What has a big mouth but doesn't say a word?
   A river.

Knock, knock.
Who's there?
Dozen.
Dozen who?
Dozen anyone answer the door?

What word grows smaller when you add two letters to it?

Add 'er' to short and it becomes shorter.

What is a ghoul's favorite food?

Ghoulash.

Two explorers were going through the jungle when a ferocious lion jumped out in front of them.

"Keep calm," said the first explorer. "Remember what we read in the book on wild animals? If you stand absolutely still and look the lion straight in the eye, he will turn tail and run away."

"Fine," replied the second explorer. "You've read the book, I've read the book, but has the lion read the book?"

Teacher: Joseph, name two pronouns.
Joseph: Who, me?
Teacher: Correct!

What is the difference between a hungry monster and a greedy monster?

One longs to eat, the other eats too long.

Knock, knock.
Who's there?
Adelia.
Adelia who?
Adelia the cards after you cut the deck.

What is the dirtiest word in the world?
  Pollution.

What do you get if you cross a giant and a skunk?
  A big stink.

What kind of house weighs the least?
  A lighthouse.

Why is it important for a doctor to keep his temper?
  Because if he didn't he would lose all his patients.

Knock, knock.
Who's there?
Francis.
Francis who?
Francis on the other side of the Channel.

What lies at the bottom of the sea and shivers?
  A nervous wreck.

What do you do with sick kangaroos?
  Give them a hoperation.

What is the easiest way to make a banana split?
  Cut it in half.

How does a witch tell the time?
  With a witch watch.

How do fish go into business?
  They start on a small scale.

Why is a dictionary dangerous?
  Because it has "dynamite" in it.

What do you call a really scary film?
  A terror-ific movie.

"What is that book the orchestra leader keeps looking at?"
  "It's the score."
  "Really? Who's winning?"

Tramp: Would you give me 50¢ for a sandwich?
Passerby: I don't know. Let's see the sandwich.

Why are elephants gray and wrinkled all over?
   Because they are difficult to iron.

What is a myth?
   A lady moth who hasn't got married.

Customer: I have a complaint.
Waiter: A complaint? This is a restaurant, not a hospital.

Teacher: Why are you crawling into class, Jimmy?
Jimmy: Because the class has already started and you said, "Don't anyone dare walk into my class late!"

Where can you always find diamonds?
   In a deck of cards.

Knock, knock.
Who's there?
Eddie.
Eddie who?
Eddie body home?

Why did the man have to fix the horn of his car?
   Because it didn't give a hoot.

Knock, knock.
Who's there?
Donald.
Donald who?
Donald Deduct.

What is the difference between a fish and a piano?
   You can't tuna fish.

Knock, knock.
Who's there?
Rufus.
Rufus who?
Rufus leaking and I'm getting wet.

Teacher: Sam, what is the outside of a tree called?
Sam: I don't know.
Teacher: Bark, Sam, bark.
Sam: Bow, wow, wow!

Why do windows squeak when you open them?
   Because they have panes (pains).

When is a green book not a green book?
   When it is read.

What is a Mexican weather report?
   Chili today, hot tamale.

*What do you call a person who thinks he has wings
and can fly?*
   Plane crazy.

Knock, knock.
Who's there?
Fresno.
Fresno who?
Rudolf the Fresno reindeer . . .

What television game is most popular with fish?
   "Name that Tuna."

Knock, knock.
Who's there?
Izzy.
Izzy who?
Izzy come, izzy go.

What does Tarzan sing at Christmas?
   "Jungle Bells."

Which fruit do vampires like best?
   Nectarines.

Susie: Mom, shall I let my hair grow?
Mom: How can you stop it?

David: Doctor, when I get my glasses will I be able to read?
Doctor: Yes.
David: Oh good, now I won't have to learn.

Who shaves the hairs off oranges?
   The barber of Seville.

Bill: Are you taking the school bus home today?
Will: No—my mom would only make me bring it back again.

Sid: My wife and I are going on a double mystery tour.
Sam: What do you mean?
Sid: Well, we don't know where we're going—and we don't know how we're going to pay for it."

Notice in an optician's window:
    IF YOU DON'T SEE WHAT YOU WANT—YOU'VE COME TO THE RIGHT PLACE.

Why did the little girl put her father in the fridge?
    She wanted ice cold pop.

Why can't you have a quiet game of cards in the jungle?
    Because there are too many cheetahs around.

Boy: Can I have a new bike, Dad?
Dad: Ask your mother, son, she takes care of recycling the money in this house.

Where can you always find money?
    In a dictionary.

What can't be used until you break it?
    An egg.

Why did Mickey Mouse go into space?
    To find Pluto.

Where do fish keep their money?
  In a river bank.

Why are clocks shy?
  Because they always have their hands in front of their faces.

When do people talk turkey?
  When they're gobbling their supper.

What does the violinist sing to his violin?
  I've got you under my chin.

How many sides does a house have?
  Two—inside and outside.

Why are chickens brown and elephants gray?
  So you can tell them from bluebirds . . .

What did the banana do when the monkey chased it?
  A banana split.

What is pie in the sky?
  A flying pizza.

Knock, knock.
Who's there?
Carmen.
Carmen who?
Carmen get it!

Knock, knock.
Who's there?
Colleen.
Colleen who?
Colleen all cars!

What is small, purple and dangerous?
  A grape with a machine gun.

Why is a robber strong?
  Because he holds up people.

How can you tell if there is an elephant in the refrigerator?
  The door won't shut.

What is the strongest animal?
  The snail, because it carries its house on its back.

What people are like the end of a book?
  The Finnish.

Knock, knock.
Who's there?
Kent.
Kent who?
Kent you tell who it is?

Knock, knock.
Who's there?
Razor.
Razor who?
Razor your hands, this is a stick-up.

Why did the windowpane blush?
  It saw the weather strip.

What did the electric plug say to the wall?
  "Socket to me!"

Where do baby trees go to school?
  To a tree nursery.

What color is rain?
  Watercolor.

What goes through water but doesn't get wet?
  A ray of light.

What did the bee say to the rose?
  "Hi, bud!"

What did the rose answer?
  "Buzz off!"

Knock, knock.
Who's there?
Police.
Police who?
Police open the door.

What did one strawberry say to the other strawberry?
  "If it wasn't for you, we wouldn't be in this jam."

What did the cannibal eat for lunch?
    Baked beings!

What is black, shiny, lives in trees and is very dangerous?
    A crow with a machine gun.

Knock, knock.
Who's there?
Luke.
Luke who?
Luke before you leap.

What disease does Count Dracula fear most?
    Tooth decay.

Customer: Waiter, this food gives me heartburn.
Waiter: Well, what did you expect—sunburn?

Teacher: Where is your pencil, John?
John: I ain't got none.
Teacher: How many times have I told you not to say that, John? Now listen: I do not have a pencil, you do not have a pencil, they do not have a pencil. Now, do you understand?
John: Not really. What happened to all the pencils?

Why shouldn't you tell secrets when a clock is around?
Because time will tell.

What did the zookeeper see when the elephant squirted water from his trunk?
A jumbo jet.

Knock, knock.
Who's there?
Anthem.
Anthem who?
You anthem devil you!

Doctor, doctor, I'm having terrible trouble breathing.
Oh, don't worry, we'll soon stop that.

Teacher: We start school at nine o'clock.
Pupil: That's OK. If I'm not here you can start without me.

What do you call a man who drives a truck?
  Ivan.

Patient: Doctor, what's the best thing to do when your ears ring?
Doctor: Answer it.

How do chickens communicate?
  By using fowl language.

If a girl ate her mother and father, what would that make her?
  An orphan.

What do you call a man who ties ribbons round sheep?
  Rambo.

Knock, knock.
Who's there?
Aunt Lou.
Aunt Lou who?
Aunt Lou do you think you are?

How long will the next train be?
   About one hundred feet.

What is a fat hippie?
   A hippo.

What do you call musical insects?
   Humbugs.

What kind of ants are found in a house?
   Occupants.

Why did the elephant swallow a mothball?
   To keep moths out of his trunk.

Knock, knock.
Who's there?
Kipper.
Kipper who?
Kipper hands to yourself.

If a man smashed a clock, could he be accused of killing time?
Not if the clock struck first.

Why does a tall man eat less than a short man?
Because he makes a little go a long way.

What's the difference between a watchmaker and a jailer?
One sells watches and the other watches cells.

First female jockey: Why are you putting on makeup before the race?
Second female jockey: You never know, it may be a photo finish, and I want to look my best.

Salesman: Good afternoon, sir, can I interest you in a memory training course?
Man: You called here only yesterday. Don't you remember?

Where do nuns go to buy their vegetables?
  Convent Garden.

Factory inspector: How many men work here?
Manager: About half of them.

What do you call a jacket that goes up in flames?
  A blazer.

What kind of birds are kept in captivity?
  Jailbirds.

An old sailor was sitting on the beach mending his fishing nets when a little boy came up to him and started staring at him.

  "What are you staring at?" asked the old sailor after a while.

  "My dad says you're an old sea dog," the little boy replied. "I'm just waiting for you to bark."

Why is a snake clever?
  Because you can't pull its leg.

Knock, knock.
Who's there?
Doughnut.
Doughnut who?
Doughnut forsake me, oh my darling.

Actor: I was once in a play called *Bed and Breakfast.*
Friend: Did you have a big role?
Actor: No, just toast and marmalade like everyone else.

Car dealer: This car has had just one careful owner.
Buyer: But look at it—it's a wreck.
Car dealer: The other five owners weren't so careful, I have to admit.

Why did the pilot crash into the house?
   Because the landing light was on.

Why should fat men wear gingham jackets?
   To keep a check on their waists.

What coat is wet and has no buttons?
  A new coat of paint.

Did you hear about the boy who drowned in bed?
  He fell through the mattress and into the springs.

Diner: Waiter, these eggs are awful.
Waiter: Don't blame me—I only laid the table.

Fred: How can I stop my dog barking in the front garden?
Ed: Try moving him into the backyard.

What has two heads, four eyes, six legs, and a tail?
  A horse and rider.

What do you get it you cross a hyena with a store-keeper?
  A laughingstock.

Two skeletons went to a dance. The first skeleton said to the second skeleton, "Why aren't you dancing?"
  "I've got no body to dance with," the second skeleton replied.

What has teeth but never eats?
  A comb.

Customer: Those apples you sold me yesterday were awful—they tasted of fish.
Grocer: That's not surprising—they were crab apples.

Teacher: If I've got $6 in one pocket and $19 in another pocket, what have I got?
Pupil: Someone else's coat on!

What do you call a man with a spade on his head?
  Doug.

What do you call a man without a spade on his head?
  Douglas.

What gloves can be seen, but not worn?
  Foxgloves.

Sam: I think our school's haunted, Mom.
Mother: Why's that, son?
Sam: Well, the principal is always talking about the school spirit.

What is a bee with a low buzz?
  A mumble bee.

What do you call a man who's good at carpentry?
  Andy.

What is round, purple and used to rule the waves?
  Grape Britain.

What vegetable is dangerous to have on board a ship?
A leek.

What musical instrument doesn't tell the truth?
A lyre.

Where does a sick horse go?
To the horsepital.

What do you get if you cross a clock and a chicken?
An alarm cluck!

Knock, knock.
Who's there?
Sabina.
Sabina who?
Sabina long time since I last saw you.

Where do snowmen dance?
At the snowball.

What rises up in the morning and waves all day?
  A flag.

Knock, knock.
Who's there?
Amana.
Amana who?
Amana bad mood!

When does a police dog not look like a police dog?
  When it is an undercover agent.

What is a sandwich man?
  A quick snack for a cannibal.

Where would you send a man with a great big appetite?
  To Hungary.

Why did the elephant wear glasses?
  Because he didn't want to be recognized when he went out.

What do well-behaved young lambs say to their mothers?

Thank ewe.

Knock, knock.
Who's there?
Zoom.
Zoom who?
Zoom did you expect?

How do rabbits keep their fur neat?

They use a harebrush.

Knock, knock.
Who's there?
Nana.
Nana who?
Nana your business.

What flower is the happiest?

Gladiola.

What do you call a man who likes throwing things?

Chuck.

116

Outlaw: Knock, knock.
Stagecoach driver: Who's there?
Outlaw: Hanover.
Stagecoach driver: Hanover who?
Outlaw: Hanover your money.

What kind of ant can count?
  An accountant!

What do you call a bee born in May?
  A maybe.

What newspaper do cows read?
  The Daily Moos.

What means of transportation gives people colds?
  A choo-choo train.

What cannot be seen but only heard, and will not speak unless it is spoken to?
  An echo.

Knock, knock.
Who's there?
You.
You who?
You who yourself!

Where do tough chickens come from?
From hardboiled eggs.

What is a hot and noisy duck?
A firequacker.

What kind of fish performs operations?
A sturgeon.

Knock, knock.
Who's there?
John.
John who?
John the Navy.

Knock, knock.
Who's there?
Cedar.
Cedar who?
Join the Navy, and cedar world.

Who brings the monster's babies?
   Frankenstork.

What grows larger the more you take it away?
   A hole.

Traffic policeman: Sir, are you aware that you were doing 50 miles per hour in a 30 mile per hour area?
Driver: I was only doing 35 miles an hour.
Driver's wife: I wouldn't argue with my husband, officer, he has a terrible temper when he's been drinking . . .

Tobacconist: Try one of the cigars, sir—you won't get better.
Customer: I know—I had one last week and I still don't feel well.

What did the beaver say to the tree?
  It's been nice gnawing you.

What kind of bolt is of no use?
  A thunderbolt.

Teacher: I've had to punish you every day this week, Gloria. What have you got to say?
Gloria: I'm glad it's Friday!

Parachutist: What happens if my parachute doesn't open?
Instructor: We'll take it back to the store and they'll give us another one to replace it.

Sally: Mom, a dog just bit my leg.
Mom: Did you put antiseptic on it?
Sally: No—it seemed to like it just the way it was.

Landlord: I don't want any pets, any guests, any noise, any loud music—understood?
Tenant: Yes, but I think I ought to warn you that my pen nib scratches a bit.

Mom: Sam, I thought I told you to watch for the milk boiling over.
Sam: I did, Mom, it boiled over about five minutes ago.

What would you do if your nose went on strike?
  Picket!

What was a tortoise doing on the interstate?
  About two miles per hour.

Knock, knock.
Who's there?
Oscar.
Oscar who?
Oscar silly question, get a silly answer!

What did the vampire say to the dentist?
  Fangs very much.

Why does Father Time wear bandages?
  Because day breaks and night falls.

What bus crossed the ocean?
  Columbus.

What did the mother bee say to the naughty baby bee?
  Just beehive yourself.

What happens to the actors when a ghost haunts the theater?
  They get stage fright.

What does a geometry teacher like to eat?
  A square meal.

When can cooks be said to be very cruel?
  When they beat the eggs and whip the cream.

What kind of hen lays the longest?
  A dead one.

What do people do in a clock factory?
  They make faces.

What do you get if a sheep studies karate?
  A lamb chop.

A young lady went to a fortune-teller to have her fortune told.

  "I will answer two questions for you for five dollars," the fortune-teller said.

  The young lady paid the fortune-teller but said, "Don't you think five dollars is a lot of money for two questions?"

  "Yes, it is," answered the fortune-teller. "Now, what is your second question?"

Teacher: What is a fjord?
Pupil: A Norwegian car?

What happens when you cross an elephant with a kangaroo?
  You get big footprints all over Australia.

Knock, knock.
Who's there?
Butcher.
Butcher who?
Butcher money where your mouth is.

What happened when the boy told the mirror a joke?
It cracked up.

Did you hear about the author who made a fortune?
He was in the write business.

Teacher: Give me a sentence using the words "defeat," "defense," and "detail."
Pupil: Defeat of de dog went over defense before detail.

Teacher: I told you to write this poem out twenty times because your handwriting is so bad.
Pupil: I'm sorry. My arithmetic's not too good either.

Pupil: Excuse me, but I can't see when you stand in front of the blackboard.
Teacher: I do my best to make myself clear, but I can't make myself transparent.

How does the sun affect weight?
  It makes the daylight.

Teacher: We have a new boy joining our class today. What is your name?
Boy: Hugh Herd.
Teacher: Don't be rude!

Man: How much is a haircut?
Barber: $2.
Man: How much is a shave?
Barber: $1.
Man: Shave my head, will you?

Pupil: What are those holes in the piece of wood?
Shop teacher: They are knot holes.
Pupil: If they're not holes, what are they?

Where can happiness always be found?
  In the dictionary.

Son: Dad, what would you do if you were in my shoes?
Father: Polish them.

Poet: Do you think I ought to put more fire into my poetry?
Publisher: No, I think you ought to put more of your poetry into the fire.

Mechanic: The horn on your car must be broken.
Motorist: No, it's just indifferent.
Mechanic: What do you mean?
Motorist: It just doesn't give a hoot.

Son: Dad, can you help me with my math?
Father: Yes, but it wouldn't be right, would it?
Son: Probably not!

Boy: I have an idea.
Girl: Beginner's luck!

What's the best way to hunt bear?
   Take all your clothes off!

Knock, knock.
Who's there?
Torch.
Torch who?
Torch you would never ask.

Caller: Hello, operator, I would like to speak to the king of the jungle.
Operator: I'm very sorry, the lion is busy.

Doctor: Did you take the patient's temperature?
Nurse: No, is it missing?

Why wasn't the elephant allowed on the airplane?
Because his trunk was too big to fit under the seat.

Knock, knock.
Who's there?
Scold.
Scold who?
Scold outside.

Two children were eating a large cake. The boy, Peter, cut the cake into two unequal pieces, and took the larger for himself.

"That's very bad-mannered," said the girl, Paula. "If I had cut the cake I'd have taken the smaller piece for myself."

"That's all right then," said Peter. "You've got it."

Teacher: If your father knew how badly you'd behaved today, Tony, he'd get gray hair overnight.
Tony: He'd be pleased about that—he's bald!

Teacher: Can you say your alphabet for me, Mary?
Mary: X, I, J, M, Z . . .
Teacher: Where did you learn to say the alphabet like that?
Mary: At the optician's.

Customer: Waiter, why have you got your thumb on my steak?
Waiter: I don't want it to fall on the floor again, sir.

Customer: Waiter, I've reserved a table. I'm giving dinner for all my friends tonight.
Waiter: Oh, you must be the table for two, sir.

How do you make time fly?
   Throw an alarm clock over your shoulder.

Teacher: If you add 3,462 and 3,096, divide the answer by 4 and then multiply by 6, what would you get?
Pupil: The wrong answer.

Dentist: Open wide. Good grief! You've got the biggest cavity I've ever seen, the biggest I've ever seen.
Patient: All right, you don't have to repeat yourself!
Dentist: I didn't, that was an echo.

Father bear: Who's been eating my porridge?
Mother bear: Who's been eating my porridge?
Baby bear: Who's been eating my porridge?
Granny bear: Oh, be quiet! I haven't even served the porridge yet.

What do you get if you cross a giant with a vampire?
   A big pain in the neck.

Knock, knock.
Who's there?
Owl.
Owl who?
Owl aboard.

Why do squirrels spend so much time in trees?
To get away from all the nuts on the ground.

When vampires go to jail where are they kept?
In blood cells.

How can you tune into the sun?
By using a sundial.

Knock, knock.
Who's there?
Sherry.
Sherry who?
Sherry dance?

Why don't bananas snore?
They don't want to wake up the rest of the bunch.

What do you call a man with a rabbit down his trousers?
  Warren.

What is brown, hairy and wears sunglasses?
  A coconut on vacation.

How do you know that army sergeants have a lot of headaches?
  Because they are always shouting "Tension!"

What nuts give you a cold?
  Cashew nuts.

Knock, knock.
Who's there?
Adair.
Adair who?
Adair once but now I'm bald.

What criminal doesn't take baths?
  A dirty crook.

What part of a clock is always old?
   The second hand.

What is a parasite?
   Something you see in Paris.

When does a graveyard romance start?
   When boy meets ghoul.

If fish lived on land where would they live?
   In Finland.

Why did the reporter keep a ruler on his newspaper?
   Because he wanted to get his story straight.

Knock, knock.
Who's there?
Jeff.
Jeff who?
Jeff in one ear, please speak up!

When it rains cats and dogs what do you step into?
   Poodles.

What did the electric robot say to his mother?
   I love you watts and watts.

What is the best way to win a race?
   Run faster than anybody else.

What do you call a neurotic octopus?
   A mixed-up squid.

Why do turkeys eat so little?
   Because they are always stuffed.

Why are scrambled eggs like a losing football team?
   Because they are both beaten.

Visitor: Is your dog fond of children?
Owner: Yes, but he really prefers biscuits and gravy.

Why is it always cool in a sports stadium?
  Because there is a fan in every seat.

Knock, knock.
Who's there?
Luke.
Luke who?
Luke snappy and open the door.

Where did Noah strike the first nail in the ark?
  On the head.

What has fifty legs but can't walk?
  Half a centipede.

Teacher: Which month has 28 days?
Pupil: They all have.

When was medicine first mentioned in the Bible?
  When Moses received the two tablets.

Teacher: If I write n-e-w on the blackboard, what does that spell?
Pupil: New.
Teacher: Correct. Now if I put a "k" in front of it, what do we have now?
Pupil: Canoe?

How do you serve toffee?
  In toffee tups.

Doctor: What's the problem?
Patient: I swallowed a roll of film.
Doctor: Don't worry, nothing serious will develop.

What did the man do when he got a big gas bill?
  He exploded.

What did one wall say to the other?
  I'll meet you at the corner.

Knock, knock.
Who's there?
Wooden shoe.
Wooden shoe who?
Wooden shoe like to know?

Teacher: Milly, what is a skeleton?
Milly: It's a man with his outsides off and his insides out.

Knock, knock.
Who's there?
Howard.
Howard who?
Howard you like to come out with me?

How do hypnotists get from place to place?
  By public tranceport.

1st Eskimo: That cough of yours is making you bark your head off.
2nd Eskimo: Yes, I do admit that I'm a little husky.

Walter, I'm in a hurry. Will the pancakes be long?
  No, sir. They'll be round.

How do actors travel around?
  By stagecoach.

What do you call a sleeping bull?
  A bulldozer.

How is a burning candle like thirst?
  A bit of water ends both of them.

Knock, knock.
Who's there?
Franz.
Franz who?
Franz, Romans, countrymen . . .

What did the invisible girl want to be when she grew up?
  A gone gone dancer.

Knock, knock.
Who's there?
Diploma.
Diploma who?
Diploma to fix da leak.

What kind of doctor treats ducks?
  A quack.

What is the difference between a man and a running dog?
  One wears trousers, the other pants.

What do you call the carpet installer's son?
  Walter Wall.

First man: I've heard about your wit.
Second man: Oh, it's nothing.
First man: Yes, that's what I heard!

Why did the chicken run away from home?
  She felt cooped up.

First performer: As soon as I got on that stage, the people clapped their hands.
Second performer: Yes, over their eyes.

Why did the reporter put a flashlight inside his mouth?

He wanted to get the inside story.

Knock, knock.
Who's there?
Wayne.
Wayne who?
Wayne are you coming over to my house?

Why did the cowboy ride his horse?

Because it was too heavy to carry.

Why did Batman go to the pet shop?

To buy a Robin.

Knock, knock.
Who's there?
Leif.
Leif who?
Leif me alone.

Why do bananas never get lonely?
  Because they go around in bunches.

Why are most cows noisy?
  Because they have horns.

Why is your heart like a policeman?
  Because it follows a regular beat.

Boy: Mom, do you remember that vase that you were always worried I would break?
Mother: Yes, what about it?
Boy: Your worries are over.

What three letters do people hate to write?
  I, O and U.

Have you heard about the two kangaroos?
  They lived hoppily ever after.

What did the horse say to his wife?
   Don't be such a nag!

What is mischief?
   The chief's daughter.

Susan: Did you know it takes three sheep to make one sweater?
Sally: I didn't even know they could knit.

Jimmy: Mommy, I can't go to school.
Mommy: Why not?
Jimmy: I don't feel well.
Mommy: Where don't you feel well?
Jimmy: In school.

What always goes to bed with shoes on?
   A horse.

Knock, knock.
Who's there?
Dunce.
Dunce who?
Dunce say another word.

What kind of person is fed up with people?
  A cannibal.

Dave: My brother's been playing the piano for three years.
Mike: Aren't his fingers tired?

Teacher: Are you any good at arithmetic?
Pupil: Yes and no.
Teacher: What does that mean?
Pupil: Yes, I'm no good at arithmetic.

Why is an empty purse always the same?
  Because there is never any change in it.

If a pencil and a piece of paper had a race, which would win?
  The pencil, because the paper would always be stationery.

What is the difference between an elephant and a flea?
   An elephant can have fleas, but a flea can't have elephants.

Knock, knock.
Who's there?
Turnip.
Turnip who?
Turnip the heat, it's cold in here!

What driver doesn't have a license?
   A screwdriver.

What is purple and 5,000 miles long?
   The Grape Wall of China.

Why do dragons sleep during the day?
   So that they can fight knights (nights).

Why do skeletons drink a lot of milk?
   Because it's good for the bones.

Knock, knock.
Who's there?
Stu.
Stu who?
Stu late to ask questions.

Why did the stale girl loaf of bread slap the stale boy loaf of bread?
  Because he was trying to get fresh.

What would you call the life story of a car?
  An autobiography.

Why was the photographer arrested?
  Because he shot people and blew them up.

What is an expert on seltzer called?
  A fizzician.

How do you make a strawberry shake?
  Take it to a horror film.

Why did you give up tap dancing?
   Because I kept falling in the sink.

When is a teacher like a bird of prey?
   When he watches you like a hawk.

Knock, knock.
Who's there?
Max.
Max who?
Max no difference, just open the door!

Bob: Why don't you answer me?
Tom: I did. I shook my head.
Bob: You don't expect me to hear it rattle from here, do you?

Customer: I feel like a sandwich.
Waiter: Well you certainly don't look like one.

What kind of test does a vampire take in school?
   A blood test.

How can you make soup rich?
   Add twenty-two carrots (carats) to it.

Sally: What are you going to give your brother for his birthday?
Jessie: I don't know. Last year I gave him chicken pox . . .

How do you catch monkeys?
   Hang from a tree and make a noise like a banana.

What did one pig say to the other?
   Let's be pen pals.

Why did the lady hold her ears when she passed the chickens?
   Because she couldn't stand fowl language.

Why did the golfer wear two pairs of trousers?
   In case he got a hole in one.

Two prisoners escaped from jail. One was seven feet tall and the other was four feet six. The police hunted high and low for them.

Customer: Those sausages you sold me were meat at one end and bread at the other.
Butcher: Yes, but in times like these it's hard to make both ends meat.

Piano tuner: I've come to tune your piano.
Lady: But we didn't send for you.
Piano tuner: No, but your neighbors did.

What was the snail doing on the highway?
  About ten inches per hour.

What advice can you give a fish to avoid being caught?
  Don't fall for any old line.

What is the best way to hold a bat?
  By the wings.

When does a mouse weigh as much as an elephant?
  When the scale is broken.

Customer: I want to arrange a loan.
Teller: I'm sorry, the Loan Arranger's not in.
Customer: Well, who do I see?
Teller: Tonto.

What is the first thing ghosts do when they get into a car?
  They fasten their sheet belts.

What is a panther?
  Someone who panths.

Why are people stronger on Saturdays and Sundays?
  Because all the other days are weekdays.

Knock, knock.
Who's there?
Weirdo.
Weirdo who?
Weirdo you think you're going?

What does a duck wear when he gets married?
  A duxedo.

What did the paper say to the pencil?
  "Write on!"

Knock, knock.
Who's there?
Cello.
Cello who?
Cello there.

What has two arms, two wings, two tails, three heads, three bodies and eight legs?
  A man on a horse holding a chicken.

Knock, knock.
Who's there?
Yukon.
Yukon who?
Yukon say that again.

What is yellow and wears a mask?
   The Lone Lemon.

Why is the mayonnaise never ready?
   Because it is always dressing!

Why did the jelly roll?
   Because it saw the apple turnover.

How can you tell if an elephant has been in the refrigerator?
   By the footprints in the butter.

Knock, knock.
Who's there?
Elsie.
Elsie who?
Elsie you around.

What is yellow, smooth and very dangerous?
   Shark-infested custard.

What is white outside, green inside, and hops?
   A frog sandwich.

Knock, knock.
Who's there?
Warrior.
Warrior who?
Warrior been all my life?

Why do skeletons catch cold so fast?
   Because they're chilled to the bone.

How do you fit five elephants in a Volkswagen?
   Two in the front, two in the back, and one in the
   glove compartment.

Knock, knock.
Who's there?
Stopwatch.
Stopwatch who?
Stopwatch you're doing this instant!

How can you tell if a giant is under your bed?
   Your nose touches the ceiling.

When does a man never fail to keep his word?
   When no one will take it.

What is the difference between a talkative bore and a book?
   You can shut up the book . . .

What animal has two humps and is found in the North Pole?
   A lost camel.

Knock, knock.
Who's there?
Doctor.
Doctor who?
You've just said it.

Father: Son, I see by your school report card that you are not doing very well in history. How come?

Son: I can't help it. The teacher always asks me about things that happened before I was even born.

Why did the boy throw butter out of the window?
   He wanted to see a butterfly.

Customer: And this, I suppose, is one of those hideous things you call modern art?

Art dealer: No, it's a mirror.

Customer: This coffee tastes like mud.

Waiter: Yes sir, it was freshly ground.

Knock, knock.
Who's there?
Heart.
Heart who?
Heart to hear you, talk louder.

German boy: Tell me your telephone number.
German girl: 999-9999.
German boy: All right, then don't!

Why do dentists tend to get fat?
  Practically everything they touch is filling.

What is always behind time?
  The back of the clock.

Knock, knock.
Who's there?
Sicily.
Sicily who?
Sicily question.

What did one candle say to the other?
  "Are you going out tonight?"

Teacher: Arthur, were you copying Harry's answers?
Arthur: No, sir, I was just looking to see if he got mine right.

Father: Do you find things hard to take in at school?
Son: Only school lunches.

Knock, knock.
Who's there?
Sultan.
Sultan who?
Sultan pepper.

What is yellow, soft, and goes round and round?
   A long-playing omelette.

What is a sleeping child?
   A kidnapper.

Why do elephants wear green nail polish?
   So they can hide in a cabbage patch.

Knock, knock.
Who's there?
Earl.
Earl who?
Earl be glad to tell you if you open the door.

What gives milk and says, "Oom, oom"?
  A cow walking backwards.

Teacher: Order, children, order!
Timmy: I'll have ice cream, a hamburger and fries.

Why did the turkey cross the road?
  To prove he wasn't chicken.

What was Noah's profession?
  He was an arkitect.

Why did the girl sit on her watch?
  She wanted to be on time.

Why did the naughty boy put ice cubes in his aunt's bed?
   Because he wanted to make antifreeze.

Knock, knock.
Who's there?
Ooze.
Ooze who?
Ooze in charge around here?

What do you call Eskimo cows?
   Eskimoos.

Why did the teacher wear sunglasses?
   Because his class was so bright.

Customer: This steak is terrible. I want the manager.
Waiter: Sorry sir, he isn't on the menu.

Knock, knock.
Who's there?
Ilona.
Ilona who?
Ilona Ranger.

What kind of eggs does a wicked chicken lay?
    Deviled eggs.

What makes learning to ride a bicycle so hard?
    The pavement.

Why is a strawberry like a book?
    Because it is red.

Boy: Can you tell me about the Iron Age, Dad?
Dad: Sorry, son—I'm a bit rusty on that.

Why did the man put a clock under his desk?
    He wanted to work overtime.

Boy: Sometimes I like my teacher.
Father: When's that?
Boy: When she's ill and absent from school.

First cannibal: The chief's new girlfriend looks like a real dish.
Second cannibal: Good, we can have her for dinner.

What did the chicks say to the miser?
   Cheap! Cheap!

Where was Solomon's temple?
   On his head.

Knock, knock.
Who's there?
Justin.
Justin who?
Justin time for your dinner.

What sort of meat does Dracula hate most?
   Stake.

Teacher: You look pretty dirty, Ruth.
Ruth: Yes, but I'm even prettier when I'm clean.

Teacher: Name five things that contain milk.
Pupil: Butter, cheese, ice cream, and ... two cows.

What happened when the well-known fruit threw a tantrum in the post office?
  A date stamped on a letter.

What happens if you cross a jeep with a pet dog?
  You get a Land Rover.

Woman customer: Is that meat tender?
Butcher: As tender as my heart.
Woman customer: In that case I'll take a pound of sausages.

Jim had been given a lift home from school by his next door neighbor.
  "Did you thank Mr. Smith?" his mom asked.
  Jim wouldn't answer, and his mom repeated the question. "Did you thank Mr. Smith?" she said. "Come on, answer me."
  Very reluctantly, Jim spoke at last. "Yes, I did thank him, mom, but he told me not to mention it."

Policeman: Did you see a man carrying a long ladder pass by here a few minutes ago?
Simple Simon: No.
Policeman: Did the man tell you to say that?
Simple Simon: Yes.

What children live in the sea?
  Life buoys.

Why is the longest human nose on record only eleven inches long?
  Because if it was twelve inches it would be a foot.

Knock, knock.
Who's there?
Disaster.
Disaster who?
Disaster be my lucky day!

When can't astronauts land on the moon?
  When it is full.

Where did King Arthur go for entertainment?
  To a (k)nightclub.

Knock, knock.
Who's there?
Pasture.
Pasture who?
Pasture bedtime, isn't it?

What is the easiest way to get on TV?
  Sit on your set.

Customer: Waiter, there's a button in my salad.
Waiter: Sorry sir, it must have come off when the salad was dressing.

Receptionist: Doctor, there's an invisible man here to consult you.
Doctor: Tell him I can't see him.

What is always coming, but never arrives?
  Tomorrow.

First mother: My Bertie always wanted to be a stage magician and saw people in half.
Second mother: Is he an only one?
First mother: Oh no, he's got several half-brothers and sisters.

Worried passenger: Captain, do ships of this size sink very often?
Captain: Oh no, sir, never more than once.

What is black and white and has sixteen wheels?
  A zebra on roller skates.

What do you get if you cross a cow and a pogo stick?
  A milkshake.

What would we have if all the cars in the country were painted pink?
  A pink carnation.

Sue: Why are you crying?
Pru: My new shoes are hurting me.
Sue: But that's because you've got them on the wrong feet.
Pru: But they're the only feet I've got!

Farmer: I keep my prize pig in my living room.
Lady: Isn't that unhealthy?
Farmer: My pig hasn't had a day's illness in its life . . .

Uncle: Would you like 50¢?
Jean: Yes.
Uncle: Yes what?
Jean: Yes, if you can't afford to give me any more.

Why did the robber take a bath?
   So he could make a clean getaway.

First man: I work in a clock factory.
Second man: Oh, what do you do?
First man: Just stand around all day and make faces.

What is the best way to catch a squirrel?
   Act like a nut and he'll follow you anywhere.

First boy: What's the difference between a lemon and a head of lettuce?
Second boy: I don't know.
First boy: Well, you'd be a fine one to send for some lemons!

First woman: My boy's been walking since he was eight months old.
Second woman: Really? He must be awfully tired.

Knock, knock.
Who's there?
Gladys.
Gladys who?
Gladys summer, aren't you?

Where would you get a job playing a rubber trumpet?
    In an elastic band.

What trees do fortune-tellers look at?
    Palms.

What kind of ship did Dracula captain?
    A blood vessel.

Why did the boy jump up and down on the letter?
    He heard that you have to stamp letters or the post office won't deliver them.

Knock, knock.
Who's there?
Who.
Who who?
You sound like an owl.

Why did the chicken sit on the axe?
    So she could hatch-et.

Father: Did you have any problems with the math questions?
Son: No, it was the answers that bothered me.

Who was the fastest runner in the world?
  Adam. He was the first in the human race.

Why are vampires so unpopular?
  Because they are pains in the neck.

Why are spiders like tops?
  Because they are always spinning.

Where do blackbirds drink?
  At a crowbar.

Knock, knock.
Who's there?
Harold
Harold who?
Harold are you?

Why are dentists such sad people?
  Because they are always looking down in the
  mouth.

What kind of cat swims underwater?
  An octopus.

Why did the girl put sugar under her pillow?
  Because she wanted to have sweet dreams.

What kind of eyes does Dracula admire?
  Bloodshot.

What kind of clothing does a pet dog wear?
  A petticoat.

Why do horses go on strike?
  To get more horsepower.

*What would you get if a young goat fell into a
blender?*
  A mixed-up kid.

Why did the girl stand on a ladder when she learned how to sing?
   Because she wanted to learn the high notes.

What did the fireman say when the church caught fire?
   Holy smoke!

Teacher: What happened to your homework?
Pupil: I made it into a paper airplane and somebody hijacked it.

Patient: I have a dual personality.
Doctor: Well, as this interview is strictly confidential, one of you had better wait outside.

What did the lumberjack's wife say to him?
   Not many chopping days left before Christmas.

What's the difference between an ace tennis player and a bully?
   One smashes the ball. The other bashes the small.

How do you get through life with only one tooth?
    You grin and bare it.

What did one tonsil say to the other tonsil?
    It must be summer: here comes another swallow.

What would the Swiss be without all those mountains?
    Alpless.

What's green, has six legs, and is deadly when it jumps on you?
    An angry billiard table.

Knock, knock.
Who's there?
Theodore.
Theodore who?
Theodore is closed, open up!

How do you make a bandstand?
    Take away their chairs.

Which English king had a heart transplant?
   Richard the Lion-Hearted.

What would you get if you crossed a cactus and a porcupine?
   Sore feet.

An apple a day keeps the doctor away.
An onion a day keeps everyone away.

Who snatched the baby octopus and held it for ransom?
   Squidnappers.

Jimmy: I think my ant is dead. I can't hear it breathing.
Jack: Give it a "P" and make it pant.

Father (to lazy son): You do nothing but laze around in bed all day.
Son: I'm in strict training.
Father: What for, sleeping?
Son: No, I'm applying for a job as an undercover agent.

What is out of bounds?
    An exhausted kangaroo.

What is a twip?
    Something a wabbit takes when he wides on a
    twain.

What happens when frogs park next to a hydrant?
    They get toad away.

How can you tell if a mountain is listening?
    Look at the mountaineers.

What lies on its back one hundred feet in the air?
    A dead centipede.

What do houses like to eat?
    Cement and bricks. It builds them up.

Why do they put telephone wires so high in the air?
    To keep up the conversation.

Why do firemen wear red suspenders?
  To stop their trousers from falling down.

What goes through a door but never goes in or out?
  A keyhole.

There are lots of things you can do for a headache, but I get one every time I try to think of them all.

Which letter of the alphabet is drunk?
  The wobble-you.

Policeman: Mrs. Jones, your husband has just been run over by a steam roller.
Mrs. Jones: Slip him under the door, I'm in the shower.

What's got feathers, fangs and swims?
  Count Duckula.

How does the ice cream man go to work if his van breaks down?
  By icicle.

What do you get if you cross a chicken with a kangaroo?
  Pouched eggs.

Fred: What were you in the army?
Ed: A desserter.
Fred: You mean you ran away?
Ed: No, I worked as a pastry chef in the canteen.

What's the difference between an elephant and a doughnut?
  You can't dip an elephant in your coffee.

What is pigskin mostly used for?
  Holding pigs together.

Boy: Did you hear about the rope joke?
Girl: No.
Boy: Just skip it then.

Grown-up: Hey, you mustn't pull the cat's tail.
Boy: Don't yell at me, I'm only holding—the cat's doing all the pulling.

Why should you never swim on an empty stomach?
  It's easier to swim in water.

How does Jack Frost travel?
  By icicle.

Why is a leopard easy to see?
  Because he is always spotted.

What is greater than God, worse than the devil, the dead eat it, but if you eat it you'll die?
  Nothing.

What do ghosts eat for dinner?
  Spooketti.

What bird is like a gulp?
  A swallow.

If the crook in your elbow is sent to jail
And inside safely put,
Surely the calves in your legs
Can feed on the corn on your foot?

When is a cigar like fish?
  When it is smoked.

A man had forgotten the combination that would
unlock his safe. He was carrying the heavy safe
down the street to the locksmith's shop when he
accidentally bumped into someone. "Why can't
you keep your money in your wallet like
everyone else?" snapped the stranger.

A hunter and trapper named Auld,
Boasted that he'd never been mauled:
He could face a wild bear
And not turn a hair—
You see, he was perfectly bald!

Boss: Everything in the factory is electrically operated.
New employee: Yes, even the salary gives you a shock!

If you want to make money, crush a five dollar bill, open it up again and you will find it in creases (increases).

First termite: How's life these days?
Second termite: Same as usual . . . boring.

What did the rug say to the floor?
    Don't move! I've got you covered.

176

Patient: I find it difficult to tell the truth.
Psychiatrist: Don't worry. Once you get on the couch you'll find it very hard to lie on.

First lady: My husband certainly sticks to his hobby.
Second lady: Oh, what's that?
First lady: Watching TV. When it's on, he's glued to the set.

Why do artists sign their pictures?
So that people can tell the top from the bottom.

Young man: I've come to ask for your daughter's hand.
Father: Sorry, you'll have to take all of her or it's no deal.

Customer: I want to withdraw some money.
Teller: Can you identify yourself?
Customer: (Looking in a mirror) Yes, it's me all right.

Boy: How's your father getting on with his new dairy farm?
Girl: All right, but he makes all the cows sleep on their backs, so the cream will be on top in the morning.

Anybody who boasts about his ancestors is admitting that his family is better dead than alive.

Customer: Waiter, where's the rum in this rum pie?
Waiter: Well, would you expect to find a dog in a dog biscuit?

What begins with "P", ends in "E", and has thousands of letters?
    The Post Office.

What was the most difficult thing for a knight in armor to do?
    Scratch himself.

Did you hear the story about the man who changed his address after forty years?
  It was a moving tale.

First goat: Who's that little goat over there?
Second goat: Oh, that's my kid brother.

What's the difference between a squeaking hinge and eggs for breakfast?
  One begs to be oiled, the other's eggs to be boiled.

Man: Have you got any mail for me?
Postman: What's your name?
Man: You'll find it on the envelope.

First man: Who do you think you're pushing?
Second man: How many guesses do I get?

What did the calculator say to the mathematician?
  You can count on me!

Knock, knock.
Who's there?
Jewel.
Jewel who?
Jewel remember me after you see my face.

First boy: What do they do with doughnut holes?
Second boy: They use them to stuff macaroni.

Teacher: What are the smaller rivers that make up the Nile called?
Pupil: The juve-Niles.

In a raid on a supermarket this weekend, thieves stole thirty sacks of carrots and 200 cigarettes. Police ask the public to be on the lookout for a rabbit with a bad cough.

Teacher: I asked you to write an essay on cheese last night for your homework. Where is it?
Pupil: I did try, but the cheese kept blocking up the tip of my pen.

Bob: I'm writing a letter to my friend Bill.
Rob: But you can't write properly yet.
Bob: That doesn't matter—Bill can't read.

What do you call two spiders who have just got married?
  Newlywebs.

How do you start a flea race?
  One, two, flea, go!

Why is a cow in a kitchen like a house on fire?
  The sooner it's out the better.

There was a young girl called Ann,
Who fried her goldfish in a pan;
Adding salt and then pepper
Didn't make it taste better—
And then she was sick over gran.

What do bees buzz at?
  A buzz stop.

How do you weigh a whale?
  Go to the nearest whale weigh station.

Why did the horse cross the road?
  Because it was the chicken's day off!

Teacher: Jason, why are you late for school every morning?
Jason: Every time I come to the corner I see the sign that says "school go slow."

It's better to find a hair in your soup than soup in your hair.

My great aunt was so ugly that they hung her up and kissed the mistletoe.

What's the difference between here and there?
  The letter T.

What has twenty heads but no brains?
  A book of matches.

Did you hear about the cannibal who toasted his mother-in-law at the wedding breakfast?

When is the best time to milk a cow?
  When she's in the moo-d.

Who is the thirstiest person in the world?
  The one who drinks Canada dry.

Knock, knock.
Who's there?
Major.
Major who?
Major open the door didn't I?

Why is a cloud like a jockey?
  They both hold the rains.

Where do pilots keep their money?
  In air pockets.

Why did the banana go out with another banana?
  Because it couldn't get a date.

What are dogs' coats made of?
  Mutt-terial.

When is a river like the letter T?
  When it must be crossed.

Why does a man with very little money buy a short coat?
  It will be long before he gets another.

When is a stray dog most likely to enter a house?
  When the door is open.

Which tree does everybody carry in their hand?
  The palm.

Do you know how long goats should be milked?
  Same as short ones.

Why doesn't a bald-headed man need keys?
  Because he has lost his locks.

185

Father Lion (to young cub): Son, what are you doing?

Lion cub: Chasing a hunter around this tree.

Father Lion: How many times have I told you not to play with your food.

Why did the little boy keep his bike near his bed?
  Because he was tired of walking in his sleep.

Why did the boy take a ladder to school with him?
  To help him get into a higher class.

What is an astronaut's favorite food?
  Launcheon meat.

When does a driver never break the speed limit?
  When it's a screwdriver.

What do cannibals play at parties?
  Swallow the leader.

Patient: What can you give me for my liver?
Doctor: A pound of onions.

What do you get if you cross a centipede and a parrot?
  A walkie-talkie.

A man bought a new hearse. Everyone crowded around to admire it.
  Then one man called out, "Your car is great, everyone is dying to have a spin in it."

Bill: But what makes you think your wife is getting tired of you?
Will: She keeps wrapping my lunch in a road map.

Pat: My mom's hobby is playing tennis. What's your mom's hobby?
Nat: She has two—knitting and swimming.
Pat: I bet her yarn gets soggy, doesn't it?

A woman walked into a shop that sold musical instruments and asked to look at a large piano.

"This piano must be very old," she said to the salesman. "They keys are all yellow."

"Oh, no, madam," said the salesman. "The piano isn't old, it's just that the elephant was a heavy smoker."

What do you call a man who lives in a back street?
   Ali.

What do you call a man who gets walked all over?
   Matt.

What do you call high-rise apartment houses for pigs?
   Styscrapers.

How did the Vikings send secret messages?
   By Norse code.

How would you feel after a free lunch in a vine-yard?
   Grapeful.

Teacher: The ruler of Russia was called the Czar and his wife was called the Czarina. What were the children called?
Pupil: Czardines.

Teacher: I hope I didn't see you looking at Bob's paper.
Pupil: I hope you didn't too.

Knock, knock.
Who's there?
Adolf.
Adolf who?
Adolf ball hit me in the mowf.

Knock, knock.
Who's there?
Dummy.
Dummy who?
Dummy a favor and get lost.

Customer: I'm sorry, but I've had an accident with this salad.
Waiter: What's the trouble, sir?
Customer: My knife slipped and I cut this caterpillar in half.

If athletes get athlete's foot, what do astronauts get?
  Missile toe.

Which mouse was a Roman emperor?
  Julius Cheeser.

Did you hear about the man who sat up all night trying to work out where the sun went when it went down?
  It finally dawned on him.

What do you call a baby rifle?
  A son of a gun.

What do you call a man who swims the Channel twice without taking a bath?
  A dirty double crosser.

Three men were under one umbrella, but none of them got wet. How did they do it?
  It wasn't raining.

Customer: Waiter, I'm still waiting for the turtle soup I ordered.
Waiter: Well, sir, you know how slow turtles are.

Mom: What did you do at school today?
Mark: We did a guessing game.
Mom: But I thought you were having a math exam?
Mark: That's right . . .

Why did the cat join the Red Cross?
   It wanted to be a first aid kit.

Why are barbers always early?
   Because they know all the short cuts.

Jenny: Is there anything worse than being with a fool?
Janey: Yes, fooling with a bee.

Knock, knock.
Who's there?
Ears.
Ears who?
Ears another knock, knock for you.

Doctor, Doctor, I feel like a bar of soap.
  That's life, boy.

Patient: I don't feel well. I keep going hot and cold, and can't remember things.
Doctor: Do you think you have flu?
Patient: No, I came on my bike.

Why is it dangerous to put a clock at the top of the stairs?
  Because it might run down and strike one.

What are the best kites made of?
  Flypaper.

If someone plays a trick on you, how can you find him out?

Go to his house when he isn't in.

What is the difference between an orphan, a bald head, a mother ape, and a prince?

An orphan has nary a parent, a bald head has no hair apparent, a mother ape is a hairy parent, and a prince is heir apparent.

How do you stop a gelatin race?

Shout "Get set!"

Man to taxi driver: Can you take a joke?
Taxi driver: Of course, sir, where do you want to go?

Boy: My brother is a blacksmith in a restaurant.
Old lady: What does he do there?
Boy: He shoos flies.

Who has a sack and bites people?
  Santa Jaws.

Teacher: Give me a sentence using the words: defense, defeat, and detail.
Pupil: When a horse jumps over defense, defeat go before detail.

Why did the elf wear chocolate trousers?
  He wanted to be a brownknee.

How do you join the police force?
  Handcuff them together.

Did you hear about the man who washed his kilt?

He could not do a fling with it.

Teacher: In the exam you will be allowed five minutes for each question.

Pupil: How long for the answer?

Why is the letter C like a magician?

It can turn ash into cash.

The immigrations officer stopped a man and his wife at customs. "Can you prove that this woman is your wife, sir?" the officer asked.

"I'll give you $1,000 if you can prove that she *isn't* my wife," the man replied.

What two letters are bad for your teeth?

DK.

Lady: Will you tell that greedy boy over there that if he eats any more food he'll bust?
Waiter: I've already told him.
Lady: And what did he say?
Waiter: He told me to stand well clear . . .

Grandma: What are you going to do when you grow up, Harry?
Harry: I'm going to grow a beard, Grandma.
Grandma: What for?
Harry: So there won't be as much of my face to wash.

Teacher: How many fingers have you got?
Sue: Ten.
Teacher: What will you have if you take three away?
Sue: A useless pair of gloves.

Mom: Did you enjoy Tim's birthday party? Was there plenty to eat?
Jim: Yes, Mom, I had lemon cake, chocolate cake, cherry cake, ginger cake, fruit cake—then I had stomachache.

Writer: What did you think of my last book?
Publisher: I'm glad to hear it was your last.

Judge: How old are you? Remember—you are under oath, and must tell the truth.
Defendant: I'm 21 and some months.
Judge: How many months exactly?
Defendant: 165.

First businessman: I always see my bank manager about a loan just before Easter
Second businessman: Why's that?
First businessman: Because at that time it's always Lent.

Who has eight guns and terrorizes the ocean?
   Billy the Squid.

What lurks around the bottom of the sea and makes offers you can't refuse?
   The Codfather.

What happens when five Englishmen throw their hats into a pot of boiling water?
You get a bowler soup.

What do you call an Italian lost in the Scottish mist?
A Roman in the gloamin'.

A man was standing in the zoo, sticking his tongue out at the snakes.

"What are you doing that for?" the zookeeper asked him.

"Well, they started it!" he replied.

What do you call a woman who goes fishing?
Annette.

What do you call a man who goes fishing?
Rod.

Knock, knock.
Who's there?
Noah.
Noah who?
Noahbody knows . . .

Knock, knock.
Who's there?
Punch.
Punch who?
Not me—I've just got here.

What kind of seagull can't fly?
A bi-seagull (bicycle).

When is a sailor like a wooden plank?
When he's aboard.

What happens if an elephant drinks too much?
He sees pink men.

What did the doctor give the patient whose hair kept falling out?
    A paper bag to keep it in.

Patient: Your cure didn't work.
Doctor: Did you drink a glass of milk after a hot bath?
Patient: No, after drinking the hot bath I didn't feel like having any milk.

Jack: Did you mark the spot where there were plenty of fish?
Jill: Of course I did, I put a cross on the side of the boat.
Jack: That's stupid. What if we take another boat next time?

Why was the cannibal thrown out of school?
    Because he was caught buttering up the teachers.

Why did the sword swallower eat pins and needles?
    Because he was on a diet.

Why do carpenters think there's no such thing as glass?
  Because they never saw it.

If an egg came floating down the Mississippi River where would it have come from?
  A hen.

Michael: I lit a bonfire under teacher's chair today, Dad.
Dad: Well you can go in first thing tomorrow and own up.
Michael: But there isn't a school anymore, Dad.

Who is the best baseball player in the world?
  Batman.

What do you get if the cross a sheep dog and a bunch of roses?
  Collie flowers.

Why do some fishermen use helicopters to get their bait?
   Because the whirly bird gets the worm.

What do whales like to chew?
   Blubber gum.

Why did the whale cross the ocean?
   To get to the other tide.

What did the beach say when the tide came in?
   Long tide no sea.

Jimmy: I know where you got that tie, Johnny.
Johnny: I bet you don't, Jimmy.
Jimmy: I do, Johnny, you got that tie around your neck.

The boy octopus and the girl octopus got married; they walked down the aisle hand-in-hand, hand-in-hand, hand-in-hand, hand-in-hand, hand-in-hand, hand-in-hand, hand-in-hand, hand-in-hand. I just hope they don't grow to eight each other.

Boy: Dad, your hair's getting a bit thin.
Dad: Who wants fat hair anyway?

How do fishermen make their nets?
  They make lots of holes then join them together.

What's soft and yellow and goes around and around?
  A banana in a washing machine.

What does a monster eat after having his teeth out?
  The dentist.

Why didn't the skeleton jump off the roof?
  Because he didn't have the guts.

Who was the first underwater spy?
  James Pond.

What do you get if a piano falls down a mine?
  A Flat minor.

How do you start a teddy bear race?
  Ready Teddy Go!

Which books teach you how to fight?
  Scrapbooks.

What do Martians have for breakfast?
  Unidentified frying objects.

On which side does a chicken have most feathers?
  The outside.

What pipe never smokes?
  A bagpipe.

There's one thing I can never seem to do
without putting my foot in it.
  Oh, what's that?
  Put my shoe on . . .

What do you get if you cross a cow and a camel?
  Lumpy milkshake.

When do motorists get the most flat tires?
   When they come to a fork in the road.

A lady, visiting an orchard, was amazed at the amount of fruit.
   "What do you do with all this fruit?" she asked the farmer.
   "We eat what we can, and can what we can't," he replied.

Pupil: How can I improve my piano playing, professor?
Professor: Try playing with the lid down.

Customer: Waiter, there's a twig in my soup.
Waiter: One moment, sir, I'll call the branch manager.

Knock, knock.
Who's there?
Miniature.
Miniature who?
Miniature open your mouth, you put your foot in it.

Girl: I wouldn't marry you if you were the last person on earth.
Boy: If I were, you wouldn't be here!

Boy: What would I have to give you to get a little kiss?
Girl: Chloroform!

When Adam introduced himself to Eve, what three words did he use which read the same backwards as forwards?
Madam, I'm Adam.

What occurs once in every minute, twice in every moment, but not in a thousand years?
The letter M.

Why should you never tell secrets in a garden?
Because the corn has ears, the potatoes have eyes, and the beans talk (beanstalk).

Son: Mom, we're going to pretend to be elephants in the zoo, and we want you to help us.
Mother: But what on earth can I do?
Son: You can be the lady who gives us peanuts.

At this moment everyone in the world is doing the same thing. What is it?
Getting older.

Why did the man enjoy his work in the towel factory?
Because it was a very absorbing job.

Two men were playing chess. They played five games and each man won the same number of games. How is that possible?
They played different people.

Boss: Why do you only carry one plank at a time? All the other men carry two.
Worker: They're just too lazy to make two trips.

Why is a pencil like a riddle?
   It is no good without a point.

Which bus crossed the ocean without getting wet?
   Christopher Columbus.

Knock, knock.
Who's there?
Congo.
Congo who?
Congo on meeting like this.

What would happen if an elephant sat in front of you at the movies?
   You would miss most of the film.

What did the mother ghost say to the child ghost?
   "Don't spook until you're spoken to."

Knock, knock.
Who's there?
Dawn.
Dawn who?
Dawn do anything I wouldn't do.

What is black and yellow and goes zzub, zzub?
  A bee going backwards.

Knock, knock.
Who's there?
Denis.
Denis who?
Denis anyone?

What do you get if you cross a cow with a duck?
  A milk float.

Patient: Doctor, I keep thinking I'm an old sock.
Doctor: I thought you looked darned funny.

What's gray and wrinkled with yellow feet?
  An elephant sitting in a custard bath.

What's black and white and red all over?
  A newspaper.

Where do you take a sick wasp?
  To a waspital.

What do you get if you cross a rooster with a poodle?
  A cockerpoodledoo.

What is smaller than an insect's mouth?
  Anything it eats.

Customer: Ten mouse traps, please.
Shopkeeper: Do you want to take them with you?
Customer: Of course I do—you don't think I'm going to send the mice here to collect them, do you?

What musical instrument do you carry around with you?

Drums (in your ears).

What has three wings, three eyes and two beaks?

A bird with spare parts.

What does a ship weigh just before it sails?

Its anchors.

What room has no floors, no walls and no windows?

A mushroom.

What is a lamp post?

It's a thing that stays in the same place for years and years, then suddenly jumps out into the path of a drunk driver.

Landlady: You must pay your bill or leave, Mr. Jones.

Mr. Jones: I'll just leave, thank you—my last landlady made me do both.

Your dad's mustache is very thick, Jim.

I know—he put hair restorer on his sandwich, thinking it was sauce.

Why is a banana like a pullover?
They're both easy to slip on.

What sort of monkeys make the best wines?
Gray apes.

When is a chair like dress fabric?
When it is sat in.

Lady: Is that meat dear?

Butcher: No, lady, that meat is lamb.

Did you hear about Johnny Broadbean, the guy who made a car out of wood?
Yes, it wooden go.

What do you call a German who lives alone?
Herr Mitt.

Teacher: Give me a sentence with "antidotes" in it.
Pupil: My uncle sort of likes me, but auntie dotes on me.

Business was so quiet at the candy factory that you could hear a cough drop . . .

A motorist was having trouble with the lights on his car. He pulled into a garage and asked a mechanic to have a look at them for him. The mechanic worked for a few minutes, then spoke to the man.

"You've got a short circuit, sir," said the mechanic.

"Well, don't just stand there," said the man impatiently, "lengthen it!"

Principal: Smith, can you tell me what we would call someone who goes on and on, talking and talking, when no one is in the least bit interested in what he is saying?
Smith: A teacher, sir?

What is neither flesh nor blood, but has four fingers and a thumb?
 A glove.

Why is an island like the letter T?
 Because it is in the middle of water.

Why do bees have sticky hair?
 Because they use honeycombs.

Boy: I feel like a spoon.
Teacher: Well, just sit down and don't stir.

What's the best thing to put in a pie?
 Your teeth.

What did the bar of chocolate say to the lollipop?
  Hello, sucker.

Cuffy: Why did the man sleep under the oil tank?
Buffy: He wanted to get up oily in the morning.

Why was the strawberry worried?
  Because its father was in a jam!

Why did the girl take a pencil to bed?
  To draw the curtains.

Doctor: Well now, is your cough better this morning?
Patient: It should be. I've been practicing all night.

The teacher struggled for ten minutes to force Jim's feet into his boots. As soon as they were on, Jim spoke. "These aren't my boots," he said.
  The teacher sighed, and spent another ten minutes trying to get the boots off again. As soon as they were off she asked, "Whose boots are these, Jim?"
  Jim said, "They're my sister's, but my Mom always lets me wear them . . ."

Teacher: I want you to be very quiet—so quiet I can hear a pin drop.
Pupil: Go on, then, drop the pin now!

Bill: How are you getting on with your request for a raise from your boss?
Will: Oh, I think I'm making some progress.
Bill: Do you mean he's agreed to give you a raise?
Will: No, not exactly, but he did tell me he's said "no" for the last time.

If April rains bring May flowers, what do May flowers bring?
  Pilgrims.